Saying 'No!'

A Survival Guide to People Pleasing and Other Self-Limiting Issues

Rachel May

Saying 'No!'

ISBN 978-1-907308-45-1

First published in Great Britain by Compass Publishing 2016.

A catalogue record of this book is available from the British Library.

Set and designed by The Book Refinery Ltd.

This book is dedicated to Paul, my Bear. He has given me everything, asked for nothing and taught me the most.

Testimonials

Below are some testimonials for my work given by clients. Some testimonials are fairly short, other testimonials are longer and more heartfelt, depending on the nature of the problem. Some are based around relationship issues; others are more broad ranging. All testimonials are genuine and were sent to me personally in written form but names have been removed to protect confidentiality

Testimonials from a client with social phobia and anxiety...

"Having spent a large part of my life troubled by certain issues arising from situations in my past, that has seen me suffer from such things as depression and relationship problems amongst other things, beginning therapy sessions with Rachel has proved to be like a breath of fresh air and has proved to be one of the best decisions I have ever made in my life. The therapy proved to shed a certain light on my issues and allowed me to see these issues in a different light, such that they no longer have a negative grip on my life and the knock on effect of this is a feeling of a new and fresh lease of life along with a very positive and healthy sense of self.

The environment in which the therapy takes place I found to be very comfortable and very safe allowing for the commitment needed on my part to share and air the issues I had with Rachel, a commitment required to see the therapy through to its natural conclusion.

All in all, I would not hesitate to recommend Rachel to anyone seeking genuine help with whatever issues they feel they may have that maybe blighting their lives in one way or another. I personally strived to find answers and help for my issues for a very long time before I came across Rachel, and it was a very long time worth waiting for."

Testimonials from a client suffering with depression and anxiety...

"Rachel has given me my life. I never thought I deserved a life before I started to see her. She is honest and has made me look at myself in a truthful way. This has been hard to do but I have learnt that once you are honest with yourself and face up to what you are really like, then you can change the way you deal with things and you can change you.

It's scary because I'd been dealing with things the same way for over 30 years so to change all of that has been a major thing for me. It didn't happen over-night and I still find some things tough to deal with but I rely on Rachel less now.

The hardest part was letting go of how I thought about myself and how I fitted in to my world. It's like when you learn to ride a bike, someone to hold on to the seat until you are ready to have a go on your own. Rachel is that person for me. She has supported and guided me until I have felt ready to trust myself. I still fall off and crash now and again, but thanks to Rachel I have the tools I need to make it less painful and I am not afraid to get back on and try again.

Rachel is great because she works with you to find the answers you need, if you work things out for yourself it's easier to understand rather than someone telling you the answers.

I cannot express enough thanks to Rachel, and picking up the phone and talking to her the first time was the best thing I ever did. It's not been easy and at times I have wanted to run away from the truths she has helped me face up to. Some of the techniques may seem strange or even silly to you at the time but trust me, go with it, believe in it, because the first time you realise the technique has worked is one of the most remarkable and liberating feelings in the world!

If you are thinking of making that call, do it, and when you meet Rachel be honest, that's the key to make the changes you want. The time you spend with her is about you, and if you let go and tell her everything, even the things you try to hide from yourself, she can help you to help yourself. Good Luck."

Testimonials on Smoking Cessation...

"Hi Rachel, I was clearing out my old emails and found your website, I would just like to thank you for your expert help in getting me to quit the fags, I am sitting here typing having been smoke free for nearly 20 months, and not even touched 1. so thanks for everything, Kind regards"

CONTENTS

CONTENTS

A NOTE FROM THE AUTHOR

This book came about as a result of my own journey through life and my need to understand my behaviour and emotions, as well as those of the people I interact with on a daily basis.

Today I run an online therapy service, Hope Level Therapy, www.hopeleveltherapy.com which is for anyone who wants to explore their relationship issues in greater depth. I work with people who have problems with family, friends and work colleagues. Pretty much everyone will have to deal with a difficult relationship at some point in their life, but no one has to go through that alone.

As with many therapists, my journey began with an emotional problem that I simply could not solve. I was trapped in a vicious relationship cycle where I was jumping through hoops for the people in my life and getting nothing in return. Worse still, I seemed incapable of standing up for myself at all. I was aware that my behaviour was not in my best interest and somewhat irrational, but, try as I might, I could not jump over the emotional barriers that were preventing me from moving forward. Eventually I decided that I needed some help, because clearly I was a little bit crazy!

I decided that hypnotherapy was the best option for me because, just like many of the clients that come to see me today, I was drawn to the idea of someone else rummaging around in my head and miraculously fixing what was so obviously broken. Of course, I soon learned that hypnotherapy doesn't quite work like that, but I was so fascinated with the process and so driven to finally begin to understand my own behaviour that I signed up on a course, eventually gaining a diploma in hypnotherapy and psychotherapy. Serendipity must have had a helping hand because amid all the courses out there for hypnotherapy, I stumbled upon the Contemporary College for Therapeutic Studies, which, in my opinion, was the very best possible place for me to learn. CCST provide training over a period of time that requires a high degree of self-discovery and, as an integrated course, it teaches from a number of different psychotherapeutic theories. Its high quality of training produces therapists who are mentally prepared for therapeutic work and capable of responding to each client as an individual.

Tom Barber and Sandra Westland, who are highly regarded therapy professionals as well as tutors and directors of the college, took me on a journey of self-discovery that turned many of the thoughts I had about myself and my relationships on their head. They encouraged me to really examine my motivations in life. They also urged me to develop my own ideas and concepts, which form the basis of this book.

It could certainly be said that I've had my fair share of ups and downs in relationships. I've been divorced twice and have had a number of long-term relationships, but I have never experienced the happiness that I share now with my partner Paul. In every previous relationship, I gave far too much of myself, both in terms of how much I tried to do for the other person and how much self-esteem I sacrificed. Some of my relationships have been abusive - emotionally, mentally and, on occasion, physically. I've had to learn the hard way what makes a relationship work for a self-confessed people pleaser and I've put what I've learned into practice in order to be in the happy, equal and lasting relationship that I'm in now.

Throughout many of my previous relationships I did everything in my power to make the person I was with happy, even though it caused me distress. Being a people pleaser is about putting other people's desires first, to the detriment of your own needs. This could mean constantly relinquishing control of the TV remote, lending sums of money to a bad debt risk, dressing a particular way or disconnecting with valued friends and family on demand. The people pleaser will do whatever it takes to satisfy the dominant person in the relationship. This problem isn't just within intimate relationships, it can surface in the workplace, between parents and children, between siblings or other family members and also between close friends. This book is primarily for those who long to stand up for themselves but find themselves emotionally blocked from doing so.

Throughout the following chapters, I will discuss a range of theories; some will already be in the public domain and others will be entirely of my own construction. I use these theories in my daily therapeutic work with clients, who come from a range of backgrounds and are facing all types of issues. I don't apologise for the fact that my work and this book contains a lot of theory as to why we operate the way they do. I consider this to be essential in gaining self-awareness. When you become aware of theories, you start to see them acted out in your everyday life. This brings about a level of understanding that can relieve stress and provides the opportunity for change.

From the beginning of my journey of self-awareness, I have changed beyond recognition. I am continually moving towards greater peace and understanding in my life and yet, the more I discover, the more amazed I become regarding how astounding we all are. In many ways, we have moved far beyond the capabilities of our fellow creatures and yet we have also fallen so far behind. In developing the spoken and written word as forms of communication that go far beyond that of any other living beings that we know of, we have also allowed a rich culture in unspoken communication to fall by the wayside. In the following chapters, you will find both explanations as to why we have evolved into what we are today and guidance on how to gain the peace that comes through finding balance in your mind.

INTRODUCTION

In all relationships, whether they are with family, friends, work colleagues or the guy who sells you your morning coffee, there has to be some form of give and take. That's normal and natural. However, some people find themselves in a situation where they are consistently putting what other people want before their own needs. Whatever is asked of them, no matter how inconvenient or unreasonable it is, they just can't say no. This is people pleasing behaviour. An example of this might be to agree to lend a valued piece of jewellery to a friend even though you know they can't be trusted not to lose or break it, or may even fail to return it, or to agree to be the nominated driver on a night out for the tenth time in a row, even though it's not your turn. A more extreme case might be to stop having contact with your friends and family because your partner doesn't like you hanging around with them, or giving control of your finances to your partner because they demand it. If you see an element of pleasing behaviour in yourself or someone you care for, then this book is for you.

I find people pleasing behaviour incredibly fascinating as it can affect anyone, no matter what their age, sex, gender or religion is. Some cultures are more prone to people pleasing than others, with the British being particularly affected as they hold image and how people see them in high regard. The real problem with this behaviour is that it can cause very deep psychological stress, which may lead to anxiety, depression, anger, social phobia, panic attacks and even physical illness.

I know from experience that it can be very hard to make a conscious decision to change people pleasing behaviour because the urge to please is so strong. People who observe this type of behaviour can be left very confused as there seems to be no logical reason why the people pleaser cannot stand up for themselves. After all, 'no' is such a small word, isn't it? For the people pleaser, however, you may as well be asking them to turn the moon into cheese! There is hope, though. With some understanding and encouragement, people pleasers can slowly create change for themselves. I wrote this book to try to help people to facilitate that change and I feel a tremendous degree of excitement about being able to help so many more people. People pleasing can really hold people back and lead them to waste opportunities. Nothing would make me happier than helping people to change and take control of their lives.

This isn't one of those books where you can skip through big chunks and turn to the chapter that relates to you. I ask that you have patience and start at the beginning, because that is where all journeys should start. You may be eager to get to the bit that will help you, but I put the chapters together in such a way that if you start at the beginning, by the time you get to the bit that is most relevant to you, you will be fully armed with all the knowledge you need to tackle your behaviour head on. This knowledge will help you to not only recognise yourself, but also recognise what you need to do in order to change.

CHAPTER 1
The Way Our Mind Works

The Mind and the Brain

The human mind is a hugely intricate piece of equipment; it is recognised to possess the most complex known form of data analysis, which is packed away into a nervous system that weighs little more than 1.4kg. It has long been held that the mind exists within the brain, however, more recently, scientists have questioned whether it also exists within the rest of the nervous system.

The brain and nervous system comprise a mass of cells that are connected through their ability to send electrical transmissions to one another. The brain operates the body through the creation of nervous impulses that drive motor function (movement of muscles), or through the production and regulation of hormones via the endocrine system (chemicals that stimulate changes in the way organs and tissues function). The brain is important for the continuation of life. If it becomes damaged, life may be impaired, or even cease altogether. Modern science has produced life support systems that will replicate certain brain functions by breathing for us and pumping chemicals into our body. But without the aid of medical intervention, once the brain ceases to function, we die. Therefore, we can conclude that the brain and, in effect, the mind is in control of every aspect of our being, whether this occurs consciously or subconsciously.

The brain itself can be divided into many parts, and each part is responsible for a particular function. How each part of the brain works has been the subject of an enormous amount of analysis, including studies into how brain injury and surgery affects function and the effects of stimulating these different parts. When we compare the brains of simple life forms with our own, it is clear to see how ours has developed during evolution.

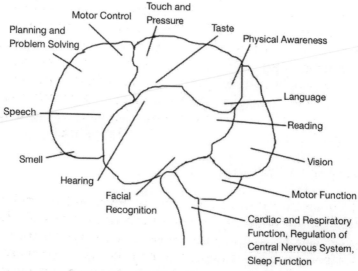

Figure 1. Areas of the brain relating to function

With a few exceptions, the most simple form of nervous system is a single nerve cord that passes through the body with ganglia (large masses of nerve cells), for each segment of the body, and a particularly large ganglion (a single large mass of nerve cells) at the head end. This sort of brain is found in very basic life forms, such as worms. The further you travel up the evolutionary tree, the more complex the brain becomes. In vertebrates (animals with a backbone), the brain is formed from a giant mass of ganglia and is recognisably divided into three parts: the forebrain, the midbrain and the hindbrain. In mammals, the forebrain has become much larger and more complicated than in fish, amphibians, reptiles and birds. This has allowed primates in particular to develop a much more complex lifestyle. It is the forebrain that holds most of the information relating to our thoughts, memories and emotions.

There are many different philosophical and psychological schools of thought regarding exactly what makes up the human mind, and even where it exists. Some theories suggest that the mind is solely located within the brain, others state that it extends down into the body via the central nervous system (modern neurological science has certainly started to explore this theory). Theories are also split regarding how the mind is structured. In truth, no one knows the answer for sure. Personally, I like to think of the mind in terms of the conscious and the subconscious, as this works well with the combination of psychotherapeutic and hypnotherapeutic interventions I employ in my work. I have formed useful analogies as to how the conscious and the subconscious operate, both separately and together.

The House and the Basement

I like to imagine the human mind as a house with a very large basement. The house represents our conscious mind and when we wander around it, we notice several things. We are aware of its temperature and the forms of energy that allow the house to function effectively, such as the lighting, the central heating and its general structural health. We are also aware of the weather conditions outside the house and the environment that it sits in, i.e. whether the house is in danger from subsidence or from a dangerous road or a noisy airport. This is very similar to our conscious mind and how it relates to our experiences in terms of thoughts. What are thoughts exactly? Well, they are the series of sounds or pictures in your mind that you are aware of; they are based on sensory input, experience, memory and belief.

We notice things about the environment that the house sits in. This information comes through the windows and doors, in much the same way that we gain information from our environment through our five senses: sight, hearing, smell, touch and taste. These sensory inputs provide the basic information that drives our actions. Very simple life forms react to this stimulation in a highly predictable way, because they process the information in a uniform manner and then act upon it. We recognise this as instinct. The more simple the life form, the more instinctively it operates. Moths are guided to light, irrespective of the source of that light, which often leads to their downfall when that light is artificially created e.g., a hot light bulb. This is because they act on instinct rather than on learned behaviour based on memory of experiences. The most basic computers work this way, which you will see if you use a calculator. It has limited function because it is programmed simply to follow a very basic set of instructions. Modern computer systems have the ability to learn through the use of artificial memory. This is leading to the development of Artificial Intelligence (AI), in which computers mimic the action of the brain.

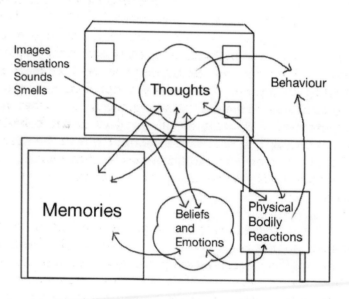

Figure 2. House and basement analogy

When we receive information through the doors and windows of our metaphorical 'house' (sensory input), as well as acting instinctively (for instance, closing our eyes when confronted with a bright light), we can act based on our learned behaviours. Sometimes we react in a way that is conscious and sometimes we react unconsciously (or subconsciously). Either way, we react based on experiences we had at an earlier time in our lives and what we learned from them. These memories therefore can create our beliefs.

For example, if we see a large dog on our doorstep we will base our actions on our knowledge of dogs and our personal experiences of them. Most people will judge the situation based on the dog's behaviour. They will base their reaction upon what they witness and will make a conscious decision as to how to react. If the dog looks friendly they may choose to go to the door and stroke it, or they may decide just to ignore it. If the dog looks angry, they might slam the door shut before the dog can gain entry. This decision is very logical and emotionally appropriate. Some people, however, will base their decision upon beliefs and memories that go against the general understanding of dog behaviour and they will slam the door shut even if the dog looks friendly. This decision doesn't appear to be very logical and it is clear that it is based on a strong emotional impulse that is inappropriate to the facts of the situation. It shows us that when confronted with a choice between logical action and behaviour based upon our beliefs, our beliefs win every time. This can be the basis for our most common anxieties, such as phobias, OCD and people pleasing behaviour. This comes from below - our subconscious.

Going back to the house metaphor, this brings us to the basement, where the subconscious resides. The basement provides the firm foundations upon which the house can rest. Without the basement, the house is structurally unsound. I consider the subconscious part of the mind to include those parts of the brain that are involved with the operation of the body beyond our conscious control, such as our digestive, endocrine and nervous systems. I like to divide the basement into two areas: the storage area and the boiler room. I guess for the purpose of this metaphor, mine is one of those big old American-style houses.

The storage area is where we keep our memories. The mind-boggling thing about this area is simply how vast it is! The storage area contains every memory of every experience we have ever had, from the first point of consciousness. This may be from the moment of birth, although some people believe we retain subconscious memories from our time in the womb. This creates a truly massive amount of information and like all massive amounts of information, not all of it is readily accessible to us. It is worth pointing out that these memories and experiences are made up of a combination of all our senses, PLUS any input from pre-existing beliefs.

Imagine watching a film where not only do you have sound and vision, you also have the ability to taste, smell and touch the experience and also feel the emotions of the characters. Mind blowing, isn't it! Yet this is exactly how your memories of experiences are built, and you subconsciously retain them all. When we are involved in a new experience, our conscious mind acts like a filter, noting the most important things about what is happening. However, our subconscious notices much more. The subtle data held within the subconscious, which helps to create our memories and beliefs, stems from a subconscious awareness of such an experience.

The storage area can be likened to a massive filing system of belongings. Like most home storage areas, we tend to keep the important and frequently used things at the front, where we can easily access them. We leave the less useful stuff further back. Right at the back of the heap, you will find the truly useless stuff, such as an old diary entry of what you had for dinner on the 6th of June when you were 10 (unless of course this was a particularly memorable occasion for you, such as a birthday). Right at the back you might also discover all of the things that you would really rather forget, such as that ugly old vase Great Aunt Agatha gave you for Christmas a couple of years ago!

Our subconscious mind stores information in exactly the same way as we store belongings. Have you ever found yourself discussing your early years with a sibling, parent or friend when they reminded you of something you used to own or a particular event in your life? This might have been something that you hadn't thought about for years and yet you suddenly recalled the memory with clarity. This is an example of just how a memory can be stored right at the back, yet the correct trigger can bring it to the front of your storage system. *desencadenante*

Sometimes, an event occurs that is similar to a past, forgotten experience in such a way that for reasons that seem inexplicable at the time, we can find ourselves in an emotional or behavioural loop. It might make no sense, yet it has a serious impact on our lives. This is because the more recent experience has triggered forgotten beliefs that are tied to a strong emotional response created by a much older memory. This concept will be explored in greater detail later, when we will look at how we develop as children. In the meantime, an example of this may be a current relationship that reminds us of a much earlier one in which we developed a particular behavioural strategy in order to avoid unpleasant confrontations. We may find ourselves reliving that behavioural strategy, even if it is in some way detrimental to our wellbeing to use it in our current situation. Some people avoid discussing serious issues with authority figures because of a past bad experience with an overbearing parent or teacher. They may be reluctant to talk to a doctor about a serious medical issue, even though the conversation would improve their physical wellbeing. *despote* *seagar*

Just as when we store physical possessions, sometimes we can misplace memories in the wrong 'storage box'. This can skew the impact of such a memory so that details become blurred, forgotten or confused. At times, a memory can be so painful for us to consciously recall that we remember less damaging aspects of what happened instead, all the while retaining the emotions of the memory itself. Imagine a small child that gets bitten by a dog on a busy street. The memory of the experience may be so distressing that the dog itself gets edited out. Yet the memory of a red bus coincidentally passing by may well be retained. The child may develop what seems like an irrational fear of buses. With no memory of the attack itself, he won't understand why he is afraid of them.

So, it's important to realise that whether a memory sits in the conscious mind or not, its existence can have a major impact on our lives. The way our memories combine and continually influence our experiences creates our beliefs, either consciously or subconsciously. These in turn can be combined with the factual information that enters our brain through our senses to influence the way we make decisions, again, either consciously or subconsciously.

Having explored the storage area, let's take a look at the boiler room. This is the place where our subconscious controls our physiology - the way our body functions. Our brain, as discussed earlier, is fully responsible for the way our body operates. Whether it's the way we digest food or the rhythm of our breathing - our brain is in control! As our subconscious is part of brain function it can have a major impact on the way that our body behaves. This can even have an impact on how we respond to illness.

A number of years ago, I was friends with an elderly gentleman who was very strong willed regarding the way he lived his life. He was well educated and very knowledgeable about current affairs. He was suffering from a form of cancer that meant that he was very immobile, but he was also highly independent. He lived alone with BBC Radio 4 constantly on for company. He had a very high regard for people who were at the top of their profession and enjoyed the mental stimulation that he gained from his beloved radio and the discussions and debates that took place on air. There came a point when his illness required a stay in hospital, much to his disgust. Although he was aware that he was very ill, he was keen to return home so he reluctantly agreed to a meals on wheels service so that he could be given a discharge date. One day, close to his 'release', a consultant stopped by my friend's bed and, during a discussion of his condition, he told my friend that he had about three weeks to live. Such was my friend's regard for the knowledge that he perceived his consultant to possess that, despite an improvement in his general wellbeing up to that point and his strong desire to return home, he totally gave up hope. He became very depressed and withdrawn and sadly passed away in hospital less than a week later.

Equally, I had a client who had been diagnosed with a very similar form of cancer and was given two years to live. She decided that she wanted to live and was prepared to do whatever was necessary to extend her life. She changed her eating habits, immersed herself in self-help manuals and concentrated her mind on positive thinking. She learned to meditate and spent many hours focused on repairing her damaged tissues. She also rejected the drugs she was given, claiming that they made her feel so ill that they were likely to hasten her demise rather than delay it. I first met her four years after doctors had given her two years to live. Her consultants were baffled at her apparent remission and lack of symptoms. My client had a strong belief in her will to live and confounded medical opinion by doing just that.

You may have read examples of how hypnotherapy is becoming increasingly popular, not only as a form of pain relief but also as a drug-free anesthetic during invasive procedures. Hypnotherapy has been used to block pain during surgery and dental treatments in situations where drugs cannot be used. This is a very impressive example of how the subconscious can have an effect on the physical functioning of the human body. The subconscious is persuaded hypnotherapeutically that neither the nerve endings in the tissues being operated on, nor the pain receptors in the brain, can feel the physical damage caused by the invasive procedure. I experienced this myself when I was hospitalised for a very distressing and traumatic medical condition. Self-hypnosis and meditation enabled me to cope with the pain and deal with my emotional distress, which made the whole experience easier to manage.

Panic Attacks and Psychosomatic Illness

A powerful example of how the subconscious can control the physical body is the experience of having a panic attack. A surprisingly large number of people suffer from one or more of the symptoms of a panic attack on a regular basis. These symptoms can cause anything from discomfort and embarrassment to the sufferer, to a genuine and very frightening belief that they might die. Panic attacks can be highly traumatic and yet they are often poorly understood by sufferers and their GPs.

A panic attack is a natural response to a situation that creates fear. This fear usually has a subconscious basis that seems to have no logical or rational cause. However, the subconscious is subtly reminded of a previous experience when there was a perceived danger. This reminder may not register in the conscious mind, leaving the sufferer with the additional fear of not knowing where their fear has come from. If the person suffers repeated panic attacks, they may find themselves in an ever-increasing cycle of distress, which I call the 'fear loop'. When this happens they may fear the fear, then fear the fear of the fear.

Experiencing subconscious fear can cause the subconscious to trigger a 'fight or flight' mechanism in the sufferer, which creates a number of physiological symptoms. This is because the body is driven toward making changes that will enable it to perform optimally in a fight or flight situation. Fight or flight is our pre-programmed way of dealing with stress, and it's learned from our ancestors who were threatened with many, more physical risks. Our bodies experience fight or flight in much the same way that ducklings know how to swim from the moment they hatch.

In a fight or flight response, our breathing rate increases to oxygenate more of our blood and our heart rate increases in order to drive the blood more rapidly to the brain and skeletal muscles involved in fighting or running away. Meanwhile, in order to conserve valuable energy, the body reduces the amount of blood to areas of the body that aren't essential to survival in this situation, so the skin may become cold and clammy. The function of the digestive system is also reduced as part of this energy saving process, so there is a risk of digested food hanging around and going bad, causing poisoning. The body jettisons this risk by inducing the desire to vomit, urinate and defecate. Even the way our brain works changes when we are in fight or flight mode. Activity in the part of the brain used for logical reasoning switches over to the part of the brain that manages instinctive behaviour, encouraging us to react quickly rather than to take time making logically considered decisions.

These physical symptoms can be very frightening to experience and many panic attack victims genuinely think that they may be dying when nothing could be further from the truth. A panic attack is your subconscious way of keeping your body alive during a perceived threat of attack. I have found that simply giving clients who suffer from panic attacks this knowledge can ease their symptoms and make their attacks easier to deal with. Once people know that their reaction is designed to be helpful, it becomes less intimidating and more manageable. Often, what people really fear is the panic attack itself. Once the fear is removed through knowledge of the process, the process itself can be manipulated or even halted.

Another example of the power of the subconscious over the body includes psychosomatic illness and avoidance. Psychosomatic illness is when a conscious or subconscious stress leads to very real and often painful physical symptoms. Illnesses that fall into this category can include: headache, backache and other muscular pain, asthma, eczema and irritable bowel syndrome, although it is important to remember that these illnesses are also triggered by genuine physiological causes and should always be investigated by a qualified doctor.

Avoidance is when a subconscious trigger creates a physiological condition that necessitates a change in normal behaviour. For example, I have helped a number of clients who have felt the need to urinate so strongly that they based their whole lives around where and when they could reach a toilet. Although this behaviour inconvenienced them in their conscious lives, enough for them to seek help, it was the result of a subconscious learning that the need to relieve themselves could also relieve them of being in an unpleasant situation, e.g., where they might be the centre of attention, have to accept unwanted responsibility or travel away from their comfort zone.

I had a client whose physical need to urinate very frequently affected his relationships, both personal and at work. He was unable to undertake long journeys for work or attend important meetings. He also found it impossible to visit his partner's family because of the long journey involved. He remembered incidences from his childhood that he felt had triggered this response and, to some degree, they had affected him. However, the real problem came when he subconsciously decided that having a weak bladder got him out of situations that he found uncomfortable because of his natural shyness. When we worked together we not only dealt with his childhood experiences, but also his personal beliefs concerning his strengths, weaknesses and abilities. Together, we helped him overcome these issues to such a degree that he was able to attempt things that he would never have tried before such as travel for work and have challenging conversations. His final task was to slowly start to increase the size of his bladder, which had naturally shrunk, as it had never had to hold a large volume of urine. With the psychological cause dealt with, he had to deal with its physiological symptom. Behaviours such as bed-wetting in teenagers and adults and unintentional vomiting in people with eating disorders are also examples of the power that the subconscious mind has to hijack the conscious self.

Emotions, Fear, Physiological Change and Dreams

When seeing the mind as a house and basement, it becomes clear that the conscious mind is very heavily dependent on the subconscious to provide it with extra information. This comes in the form of beliefs that are overlaid onto sensory input in order for decisions to be made. However, the subconscious isn't very efficient at communicating with the conscious mind, and it relies upon the three tools it has at its disposal to make the conscious mind aware of these beliefs.

The first of these tools is emotion. When we feel strong emotion, it is a result of beliefs that we hold about ourselves and other people. In general, the less familiar we are with someone, the less likely we are to exhibit emotions towards them. Of course, they may well remind us of someone who we have already experienced, in which case, we may respond to those similarities rather than to the person as an individual. Most people are familiar with the fact that abused animals, especially mammals, can be upset by people who remind them of who abused them. The trigger might be the sex or skin colour of a person or that they have a beard or wear a hat.

A human example of this might be a bad reaction to all authority figures, which was learned in childhood. This could be the result of an actual experience, or via a perceived threat. Many children learn to respond to the phrase 'wait until your father/mother/teacher hears about this' although in reality, most healthy households, these threats have no basis. Emotion in itself is a very strong force, and it may well be enough to cause a particular pattern of behaviour within us. In short, our emotions can bind us to behaviours that make no logical sense whatsoever.

The most powerful emotion that we experience is fear and this can lead very rapidly to anger as we attempt to defend ourselves from its trigger. I encourage my clients (and myself) to recognise their anger as it arises and always ask the question, 'what am I

fear → anger

frightened of?' This can take a bit of practice and it is often easier to do as a retrospective exercise at first. But once people start to explore the fear behind their anger, they are in a much better position to deal with it and learn very important lessons about themselves and how to manage their emotions. It also helps us to understand anger in others and how to respond to that, whether in a one-off experience with a stranger or with someone we deal with on a daily basis. A parent may find themselves responding angrily to a child's behaviour because, deep down, they fear that the behaviour may harm the child in some way. A person may respond angrily to their partner's choice of clothing, or the way they behave when they are out with friends, because they fear of losing control over their partner and the relationship.

When emotions are not enough, our subconscious falls back on its two other communication methods - physiological change and dreams. Physiological change is when our body responds to subconscious stimuli to create a physical need - to be removed from pain, to urinate, to vomit, etc. These physical symptoms can be much harder to ignore than emotional discomfort. I believe that this is why people who suffer from panic attacks often zone in on one particular aspect of them and subconsciously use this as a way of adapting their lives in order to avoid certain situations. The fear of needing to defecate or urinate can prevent people from going on long journeys, attending meetings or being in certain social situations. Other physiological indicators of subconscious distress can include blushing, excessive sweating, tremors and insomnia.

Throughout history, people have been fascinated by dreams. Our dreams can be funny, frightening or downright weird. Often they can have a sexual nature. This is something that the famous Austrian neurologist and the so-called 'father of psychoanalysis' Sigmund Freud based many of his theories upon. It has long been recognised that our dreams are our subconscious way of processing information about our daily lives. They can be based on everyday events or issues that might be bothering us. Dreams that have a repetitive nature can be our subconscious way of making sense of a situation or behaviour that we are fearful of.

There are literally thousands of different books and websites dedicated to offering explanations about our dreams, but the truth is that dreams are subjective and unique to the individual. Admittedly, there are certain dreams that we seem to hold in our collective subconscious – for instance, dreams about losing teeth and appearing naked in public are very common. However, bearing in mind that there are certain experiences that we will all share due to similarities in our development, it isn't surprising that we recognise them in the same way. Anyone who works with animals will know how difficult survival is for one that has lost its teeth, so it isn't any great surprise that many of us share that primeval fear of losing them – it links to concerns about wealth and security in our subconscious mind. However, a dream about snakes will mean very different things to those who have snake phobias and those who keep snakes as pets. Freud would have us believe that dreams about snakes have a sexual connotation due to their (vaguely) phallic shape, but then it seems to me that Freud believed that our every thought, conscious or subconscious, had a sexual origin!

Sometimes, we will dream about people outside of their normal context within our lives. This can leave us feeling rather bewildered and unsettled when we wake up. When this occurs, it is important to remember that often the person we are dreaming about is a representation of a concept. This is especially the case if these dreams have an oddly sexual aspect. I had an experience where a number of very dear friends descended upon me for a weekend. I had expected them to stay for a few days but soon learned that they planned to stay for well over a week. The stay went on and on and by the fifth day I was dreaming that our pet goose was being attacked by a gaggle of strange geese, and I was struggling to protect her. Bearing in mind my very private nature and the struggle I have always had with sharing my personal space, you don't have to be Freud to figure out the symbolism. As much as I love my friends dearly, my subconscious was feeling the pain caused by my lack of personal space. It was obviously pain that I had been shutting out of my conscious mind because I didn't want them to feel unwelcome!

I once worked with a lady who was experiencing repetitive dreams in which her young daughter was abducted within her house and tortured behind a door that she could not open. When we explored the dream fully using hypnotherapy, we discovered that the basis of the dream was a feeling of helplessness that came from someone she cared about being attacked. She realised that these feelings were linked to an experience that occurred during her teenage years, when an associate murdered one of her friends. The lady had never come to terms with what had happened, and felt as though in some way she should have acted to prevent the murder. This feeling of helplessness was being subconsciously played out, again with a vulnerable female in familiar surroundings. Once she was aware of the root of her dreams, we were able to hypnotherapeutically alter the dream, giving her the power she needed to confront the attacker in her dream space and come to terms with her feelings.

So, now we are beginning to understand just how complex the link is between conscious and subconscious thoughts. Many clients come to me in a state of extreme distress and by and large, they usually ask me two particular questions. The first is: 'how many sessions will I need?' As you may already be able to tell, there is no easy answer to this. Much depends on the root of the problem and how willing the client is to be open-minded and to embrace change. Any awareness, no matter how small, will start to create change and the more awareness you gain, the greater the possibility there is for change.

The other question I often get asked, directly or indirectly is: 'am I going mad?' The mental strain placed on the conscious mind by the subconscious can be so great that it does actually feel as though that person is going a little crazy. What is actually

tira y afloja
X tira la cuerda

happening is something akin to a game of tug-of-war, with the conscious and the subconscious mind on opposing sides. The conscious mind tries to follow the route of logic whilst the subconscious is driven in an entirely different direction by deep-seated beliefs. The problem is that the conscious part of our mind is much like the part of an iceberg that is visible above the waterline – it's significantly smaller than the subconscious part that sits below. Imagine these two parts in a tug-of-war. One side is ten times greater than the other. It's no wonder that the subconscious, with its emotions, physical symptoms and dreams, can overpower the conscious mind. The incongruous nature of the two parts is what causes that feeling of loss of control. The trick is to discover exactly what is bothering the subconscious mind so that it can be reassured and put in line with the logic offered up by the conscious mind.

Figure 3. The tug of war between the conscious and the subconscious

In the next chapter, we will take a look at human development from an evolutionary point of view. I consider this to be a very important part of the story when it comes to examining current human behaviour. However, I am going to touch on that subject matter just a little right now.

actos desinteresados

I am not a believer in the selfless act. I appreciate that people can and do commit acts of astounding bravery, sometimes even giving their own lives to save the lives of others. Certainly when this occurs, it appears that those individuals have been able to put aside their desire for their own survival in favour of the survival of others. However, what is happening within the subconscious mind of that individual might be a completely different battle.

We are born with a phenomenal survival instinct. It drives us away from anything that hurts us and towards anything that provides us with a feeling of comfort. For less evolved organisms, that means staying alive at all costs. There are countless stories of trapped animals gnawing off their own limbs in order to escape. However, the human mind has developed to a stage where survival includes mental and spiritual comfort as well as physical comfort. And sometimes mental, spiritual and physical comfort can be in conflict with each other.

For some people, the mental anguish of accepting someone else's death may be sufficient to override their need for physical safety. From people jumping into icy rivers to save their dogs, to people risking their lives for their religion or offering themselves up to secure the release of hostages. Let me explain further. We all seek what I like to call Ultimate Safety and Comfort. This is when we feel totally safe in mind, body and spirit. There may be times when people are willing to sacrifice their physical comfort in return for the mental or spiritual comfort that brings them closer to Ultimate Safety and Comfort. For these people, their mental or spiritual wellbeing takes precedence over their physical wellbeing, and that can lead to massive physical sacrifice. People can commit horrendous crimes in order to satisfy their own mental and spiritual needs. To them, what they do is necessary in order to satisfy a very deep personal belief and need. This does not make the need or belief right, but it is deeply compelling to the people who share it. The crimes of religious terrorists are a good example of this in action.

Mistaken Beliefs

As discussed earlier in this chapter, as we grow and live, we develop values and beliefs based on our perception of what we experience. Sometimes we are aware of these beliefs, and sometimes they sit in our subconscious. As a therapist, I know when I've hit on an unhelpful subconscious belief that has just been exposed because my client will well up with emotion. This emotion is the subconscious communicating that its needs are being heard. Although the client may find this experience difficult, it usually leads to a major realisation and shift if the client allows the process to continue (even though at the time it can be distressing for them).

The problem arises when we have conflicting subconscious beliefs, all fighting in different directions to achieve the goal of safety and comfort.

Let's take comfort eating as an example of belief-affecting behaviour. We usually comfort eat as a means of gaining a reward. Food makes a very good reward because it is something that we can enjoy just for ourselves, and it's also part of our primal need for survival. When we comfort eat, we are having a very personal experience of reward in that we don't have to share it with anyone else. This also conveniently touches our instinctive buttons, which means that we subconsciously recognise it as something that is physically good for us.

Our ancestors lived in a time when food was much harder to come by. Any opportunity to eat fat or carbohydrate meant being in a better position to survive. Animals in the wild that kill to eat often ignore the muscular parts of the kill in favour of parts like the liver, which are richer in fats and energy. Our ancestors developed taste buds that meant that eating food that was particularly rich in energy also gave a pleasant dining experience, which encouraged them to eat more of the same. The natural and evolutionary upshot of this is that fats and carbohydrates continue to be more satisfying to our taste buds. To this day, we crave fatty and/or carbohydrate rich foods above all others, even if our diet is energy rich.

When we are tired or feeling down, we turn to our food reward as a form of comfort. However, in these days of relative excess, our intake of comfort food goes beyond our physical need for calories and most people will feel some guilt about managing their weight effectively. The short burst of pleasure you get from the food reward is rapidly followed by a feeling of dissatisfaction with yourself, as the subconscious part of you that judges on appearance (especially your own) takes over. So you go from comforted straight back to feeling low. How do you deal with this low feeling? That's right, you comfort eat, and so the cycle goes on. When this cycle gets out of control, particularly in people who have a unhealthy expectation of how their body should look, it can lead to low self-esteem, binge eating and self-induced vomiting, etc. We will deal with mistaken beliefs in more detail in later chapters, but for now, it can show how two separate subconscious motivators can be strong in their desire to achieve comfort and safety and, that by working against each other, they can actually take someone to a very unsafe place indeed.

This confusion around our beliefs can be seen in all our behaviours, from the way we act in relationships to how we complete, or fail to complete, tasks. Our upbringing moulds our beliefs in such a strong way that we find certain ones very hard to shake off as adults.

On my own journey, I uncovered a 'mistaken' belief that was really holding me back. At some point in my childhood, I must have found that when I was being perfectly behaved, or at least not being naughty, I was rewarded in some way. Maybe I received praise, maybe I sensed gratitude for my good behaviour - I'm not absolutely sure. I had developed this behaviour in order to seek reward and had ended up with the subconscious and mistaken belief that in order to feel safe and comfortable, I needed to be needed: to be the perfect companion, child, partner. I found myself searching for ways within my relationships where I could create a situation in which I was as perfect as possible in the eyes of the other person, often in such a discreet way that the people around me weren't even aware of many of the things that I did for them. This became an issue when people took for granted that I was someone who 'did stuff' and therefore expected me to do everything without reward. I became a people pleaser!

In my more unhealthy relationships, I would find that those people would even get angry with me, expecting me to maintain these very high levels of support in impossible situations. I would find myself driving myself harder and harder to produce results, to the detriment of my own wellbeing. I discovered this about myself as I was coming out of a particularly unhealthy relationship that had drained me almost to the point of total breakdown. As I attempted to break away from this person, I would find myself coming up with excuses to do just a little more for them. In some way, for me, breaking away had been a sign of my own failure. Eventually, I realised that I was maintaining this unhealthy relationship, which was causing me untold amounts of distress, in order to feed my own need for being recognised as perfect. If I left, I had failed. Once I realised this, I was able to break away, although even with this new insight, I found it very hard to do. I was able to see that a powerful subconscious urge was incongruent with my other needs, and yet it was so strong that it drove me to attempt to please someone whom I now know (because of their own subconscious drivers) could never allow themselves to be pleased by another person's actions. Once we start to question, we never stop learning about ourselves.

Here I've made a common list of mistaken beliefs - maybe you can relate to some of them:

- I cannot be alone
- I need to be needed
- I must achieve perfection
- My needs have no value
- I am stupid/ugly/fat
- I must please others, no matter what
- Authority is scary
- Other people are always right
- Saying no is bad

- All spiders/dogs/birds, etc., are threatening
- My parent/spouse/sibling/child/friend/colleague has needs that are more important than my own

Dealing with Anger and Fear

incomodidad

The result of going against beliefs is usually discomfort, which is created by the subconscious mind to let you know that you are about to do something potentially harmful. This discomfort may even take the form of fear. Fear is our natural reaction toward something that we have consciously or subconsciously learned to be harmful to our comfort and survival, and it can be seen in many of the more sentient life forms. Our natural response to fear is to run away but, in today's culture, that is often inappropriate or impossible. When flight is no longer an option, we will turn to the next available one - fight.

Clients often come to me with anger issues. They appreciate that their anger is inappropriate, and even harmful to others, and yet they don't know where it comes from or how to deal with it. As discussed earlier, my first task when dealing with this problem is to enable the client to see that their anger stems from subconscious fear. Anger is a natural part of the fight or flight mechanism. When flight is not an option and you prepare to 'fight', anger is often a result, although this process is so rapid that the fear itself isn't consciously noticed.

When finding yourself getting angry, recognising your anger and your fear can be an important way to stay safe. First of all, check that you are not at risk of physical harm. If you or someone around you is getting angry and you recognise that you may be in real danger, attempt to remove yourself from the situation or diffuse it as quickly as possible, even if that means losing face in the short term. Many cases of domestic violence could be prevented if the anger on the part of the perpetrator didn't escalate. However, this requires a depth of self-development and understanding that the perpetrators of domestic violence never reach. Sometimes the answer to our anger is clear and can be dealt with very effectively. When the answer isn't clear and there is no obvious danger, then there is still no point in remaining angry. Instead, take some time out and play the 'what if' game. In your own head, follow the scenario out to its natural conclusion, as though the other person/people involved continued with their current behaviour. Sometimes this exercise can reveal the root cause of the fear and often it can help to expose a subconscious and mistaken belief.

I once felt very angry with a partner for failing to take his dirty plates to the kitchen. Instead of playing out the 'what if' game in my head, I played it out in real life by refusing to pick up after him. This went on for several days, with the pile of plates growing ever higher and the discarded food developing its own mini-ecosystem of mould and bacteria. Eventually, of course, I had to clear away the mess myself. Apart from the environmental health risk, we were in danger of running out of plates! What I discovered about myself in the process was that although I didn't like being taken for granted, I had already allowed my partner to expect me to do everything for him. He genuinely believed that it was the job of any woman in his life to pick up after him, and my need for self-respect was desperately at odds with my belief that in order to be loved, I had to be his perfect partner. In reality, my partner simply didn't care about his living space. Frankly, he didn't give a damn whether the plates were removed or not, but I cared because of what the risk of not clearing them away meant to me - ultimately that I might not be loved. *en desacuerdo*

A client of mine found herself getting angry in work related social functions, and this was exacerbated by alcohol. She recalled a particular encounter where she had become angry with a co-worker and had been rather disparaging about their fidelity. She admitted that her comments had no basis in fact and was very confused about what made her blurt them out. When we explored the situation fully and looked at her working experiences with this person, we discovered that her only issue was the length of time that her staff would take when sent on an errand to this person's department, as they would get distracted. She feared that her co-worker had gained more loyalty from her staff than she had, and this gave her a subconscious belief regarding their faithfulness, even though she consciously knew that they could be trusted. This conversation led to many others regarding the subject of loyalty, which unearthed a number of occasions when my client had become angry at a perceived threat toward someone's loyalty to her.

It is worth remembering, especially in an argument, that other people's anger comes from fear too. Next time someone is defensive or aggressive toward you, even passively, remember that they may be responding to a subconscious belief that holds them in its grip. A lack of self-awareness on someone else's part really doesn't need to spoil your day!

Summary

In this chapter we:

- ✔ Learnt how our brain controls the way our body operates.
- ✔ Looked at the conscious and subconscious mind, and how they work.
- ✔ Explored how memories are created and how they affect the way that we behave, make decisions, feel physically and respond to illness.
- ✔ Learnt what a panic attack is, how it affects us, and how we can regain control.
- ✔ Discovered how the subconscious can cause illness and affect bodily functions.
- ✔ Explored how the subconscious communicates with the conscious mind through emotions, physiological change and dreams.

- ✔ Learnt how anger is based in fear and how we explore our fear in our dreams. *a hular*

- ✔ Discovered how the subconscious can override the conscious mind, and the importance of congruence.

- ✔ Considered the selfless act and how our mental, physical and spiritual selves can be in conflict.

- ✔ Discovered how our mistaken beliefs can cause us to behave in ways that may be dangerous for us and can lead to people pleasing behaviour.

In the following chapter I will explain just how we got to be like this in the first place.

CHAPTER 2
A Brief History of Human Development

Evolution

Now that we have a basic understanding of the way the mind works, I think it's important to explore just how this situation came about. We are not designed to live in the world we do. In fact, human kind hasn't evolved a great deal since the early ages when we lived a hunter-gatherer lifestyle.

Evolution depends upon accidental genetic mutations creating an advantage in the organism they occur in. This advantage makes it easier for the organism to survive, and thus continue to pass this mutation on. We study evolution and genetic manipulation in animals such as fruit flies and mice because they have very short life cycles. This means that they can reach reproductive age in a matter of days or weeks. They also have large numbers of offspring, so genetic mutations are more likely to be seen with each reproductive cycle.

Humans, on the other hand, have much slower reproductive cycles, usually with only one offspring born in each cycle and only a few offspring born to each individual. This means that evolution occurs much more slowly in the human race. One of the most obvious ways in which humans have evolved beyond animals can be seen in the size and complexity of our brains - a reflection of the deep cultural and technological advances that we have made over many thousands of years.

So how does this tie in with understanding our modern day mental health problems? As much as we have made massive cultural and technological leaps forward, our bodies are still pretty much as they were 20,000 years ago. We may have grown a little taller and a little less hairy as a response to our greater ability to access resources, but our hormones, nervous system and instinctive responses remain much the same. The fight or flight mechanism discussed in the previous chapter is instinctive within us from a time when attacking or fleeing were the only sensible responses to danger, and pretty much 'covered all the bases'. These days, the fight or flight response is rarely appropriate, and yet our body acts in accordance with instinctive subconscious triggers that seem beyond our control.

Prehistoric people lived a much simpler life. Their needs were much more immediate and their idea of long-term usually translated as one cycle of the seasons. They relied on their strength and agility, not only to hunt for food and to protect against animals but also to settle disputes within and between human groups. They also relied on their ability to learn, not just the conscious learning of how to build a shelter and prepare food but the subconscious learning that came from experiencing extreme emotions in certain situations. If a particular plant made our prehistoric relatives ill, the stress of that illness would help to impress on them the danger of eating that plant again.

We still experience this subconscious learning today. An example from my own life is that I cannot stand blackcurrant jam. This relates to when I was young and I had an infection that led to very painful cellulitis in my leg. I was prescribed some very large capsules of antibiotics that I just couldn't swallow. In desperation, my mother broke a capsule open and mixed the contents with some blackcurrant jam. The taste and experience was so unpleasant that I immediately threw up. To this day, the smell of blackcurrant jam makes me heave. You may know someone who has over-indulged in a particular alcoholic spirit that made them ill – you'll find them unlikely to go near that spirit for a quite a while!

Neurolinguistic Programming is a series of techniques that were developed by Richard Bandler and John Grinder in the 1970s. One aspect of NLP describes 'anchoring', a situation where memory recall, changes of emotional state or other responses become 'anchored' to a certain stimulus.

We anchor things all the time. Smells are often some of the strongest anchors we have. Regarding my experience with the blackcurrant jam, I have subconsciously anchored the smell of this tasty preserve with the experience of being sick. Even though the jam itself was not the problem, my heightened emotional state at the time caused me to link the smell with the desire to be sick. Have you ever walked past a stranger who is wearing the same aftershave or perfume of your first love? The smell takes you straight back to a series of emotional memories that may leave you feeling as though they have only just happened.

This is a very important behaviour, which was designed to keep us alive when the world was dangerous in a different way. Anchoring the smell, taste or appearance of a particular berry or insect to becoming violently ill would have been a strong reminder to prehistoric man that they needed to avoid all contact with similar items in future. We have kept this ability to link a sensory event with a strong emotion but now it applies to many different things. Phobias towards foods can sometimes be linked to choking experiences in childhood. In fact, I once worked with a lady who had experienced a choking experience with a certain type of drink and she was extremely afraid of trying that drink again.

It isn't just things from our physical world that we anchor; we also anchor bad and good emotional experiences. A bad experience at school or work can make it very difficult for some people to put themselves through similar situations, even though these new circumstances pose no obvious threat. These subconsciously-learned experiences can lead to shyness, loss of confidence and irrational fear in all kinds of situations. Sometimes, these anchors

interrumpidas,

can be disrupted using NLP techniques within hypnotherapy. However, the anchor is sometimes so complex that it needs deeper work to break down the beliefs involved. Anchored behaviours and beliefs can become so entwined with our core being that it is hard to find where the anchor ends and the belief begins.

I had a client who'd had a bad experience when eating out with a relative as a child. She had choked on a piece of food and had become the centre of attention though the concern of the people around her. This embarrassing experience had created a food related anchor that made it virtually impossible for her to eat in company. This problem slowly escalated as she grew up, until she found it hard to even leave the house alone. Her father had always been a strong and supportive figure in her life whereas her mother had undermined her confidence. This was purely accidental on her mother's part, as all she was trying to do was protect her daughter from her own perceived fears of the world. However, combined with her food-related issues, this lack of confidence had made my client's life very difficult indeed. When we met she was highly reliant on her partner to help her through life and to deal with her panic attacks when they occurred. Although supportive, her partner was enjoying the role of the protective male who could sooth his partner's fears. Unfortunately, this created a synergistic relationship between them. She was rewarded for her panic attacks by the feeling of comfort and safety that she craved when her partner came to her rescue and her issues with food ensured the continuation of the panic attacks. Whilst this synergistic behaviour was allowed to continue, my client's problems got worse. However, she was very intelligent and with the right guidance and a little hypnotherapy, she was able to see the situation as it really was and take an active role in her own recovery. Within three months, she was free of panic attacks and able to live a normal lifestyle. Together, we explored her relationship with her partner and looked for ways that they could both continue to enjoy their partnership in a far more healthy way.

Child Development

The way child development evolved in prehistoric times has a great impact on the way we behave now. In fact, we share many of the same behavioural traits with our ancestors. For example, unlike some herbivores such as sheep and deer, whose young are capable of running from danger within hours of birth, human babies are totally vulnerable when they are born and are unable to properly take care of themselves for many years. This leaves them at risk for a significant amount of time, a time that allows for deep bonding to occur between the child and its adult carers.

At the point of birth, human babies have some instinctive behaviour, but are yet to acquire any learned knowledge. They have to rely on the adults around them, not only to keep them safe but also to teach them what they need to know in order to survive. This is why human children believe what their carers tell them, and will trust them with their Ultimate Safety and Comfort, even when their carers may put them through daily discomfort.

When a child is born, it instinctively knows that it is reliant on its carer for its wellbeing, and it watches them carefully for an indication of the safety of its environment. Children fear abandonment by a carer because ultimately this could lead to their death. We exploit this behaviour in our children, and we are not the only species to do so!

In the wild, young bull elephants live with the matriarchal herd until they are big and strong enough to join a male herd. These young 'teenage' males can get to be a handful as they start to practise throwing their weight about. The way the matriarch deals with this is to expel them from the herd for a while until they show signs of submission and an awareness of their behavioural boundaries. In effect, what she is saying is: "stay out there, outside of the protection of the herd, with all the predators that might eat you, until you can behave in a way that is socially acceptable."

[handwritten: comply - cumplir / comply with my expectations]

[handwritten margin: Conformidad]

The fear of danger is usually enough to pull the young male into line, at least until he is so old that predators are no longer a threat.

If you're are a fan of the hire-a-nanny style reality TV shows that are very popular at the moment, then you will be familiar with the concept of the 'naughty spot'. This is the method of seeking compliance from a misbehaving child by making it stay in one location until it behaves, and it uses exactly the same technique adopted by elephants. Effectively, the carer is ostracising the child from the social group until it is willing to conform to social norms and behave within appropriate behavioural boundaries.

As children, the fear of abandonment by our carers exists on a subconscious level and this is usually enough to make us want to please them by behaving in a manner that they find more acceptable. This might seem like a rather cruel trick once you are aware of the subconscious, psychological implications (i.e. behave how I want you to or you might die), but it is a very effective way of making sure that our children conform to our social needs.

In prehistoric times, a misbehaving child could threaten the safety of the whole group, so compliance was extremely important. These days, a misbehaving child could unsettle the family unit to the point where it falls apart. The threat is very real in both situations. This is why ideally the naughty spot needs to be within sight and sound of the rest of the group. This allows the child's feeling of abandonment, whilst teaching them how properly functioning social groups work. They can learn safe in the knowledge that a place in the group still exists for them.

This fear of abandonment might provide us with a useful childcare technique, but it also has major implications on the way we grow psychologically. In situations where a child loses one or both parents, either through death or separation, the impact on them can be severe. The child's worst subconscious fears have been realised and he or she feels, albeit subconsciously, that death may be imminent. This can leave a child with deep-seated fears – even anger - that may well follow them into adulthood and affect the way that they relate to others. Childhood bereavement may lead to an inability to form healthy relationships through lack of trust, leading to the person concerned either pushing away people who get too close or becoming obsessive and paranoid about a partner's behaviour.

Adults sometimes use a child's fear of abandonment to help them get away with abusing them. Children who have been abused by their carers often still carry a bond of love for them because they subconsciously also see them as their saviours. This is a clearly misguided belief that causes problems for people who are trying to identify abuse as the child may try to protect their abuser.

Learning and Logic

As we grow, we learn from our environment. In very small babies, this is simple and involves experiencing heat, cold, hunger, thirst, discomfort and pain, etc. However, as we grow and start to interact with our carers, we start to learn from example. This is because we instinctively know that in order to have the best chance of survival, we should emulate the behaviour of an adult member of our species that has successfully reproduced. The best and closest example we have of this is our own carer. As mentioned earlier, when we are infants, we totally trust and believe our carers. This is because we are dependent upon their knowledge - as yet, we have none of our own to fall back on. So what the carer says goes!

We learn many of our most fundamental and deep beliefs in this way. We have two ways of learning from an adult - by hearing what they tell us and by how they behave themselves. If a child watches a parent when the parent is scared of something (i.e. a spider), then the child will also learn to be afraid of it, not because the spider threatens them but because it threatens the adult. If the adult shows signs of fear, then the child knows that its own life may be in danger. So we learn a lot from adults, not just by how they interact with us but also by how they interact with the world and also with others. You may be aware of the concept that boys marry their mothers and girls marry their fathers. Whilst this is not always strictly true, the basis comes from the way we interact with our parents and how they treat each other when we are children. This will be discussed in greater depth in a later chapter.

An important step in child development comes with being able to process logic. This process is gradual and typically becomes more pronounced between the ages of six and eight. Children younger than this age often think in a very illogical way. A perfect example of children beginning to process logic is how they may start to question the existence of Santa Claus. To a very young child, it's perfectly acceptable to believe the adult who tells them of a magical man who not only knows the name, address and behavioural attitudes of every child in the world but can also carry presents for each and every one of them in a sled towed by flying reindeer, simultaneously delivering them on one night of the year. The fast developing logic in children aged (roughly) between six and eight will lead them to begin to question this impossible scenario.

This new ability to process logic also enables the child to question the meaning of their existence. Often around this age, children start to worry about death. Sometimes they will share their concerns, but, more often than not, they will lie awake at night creating a new kind of night terror from their own logical realisation that if all things die then so, eventually, they will too. Children at this age are not equipped with the knowledge and understanding that death is a result of illness or accident, and they fear that it can reach them at any time. Thoughts of sleep remind them of this, meaning they are most fearful at bedtime. Prior to this age of logical discovery, children make all types of illogical connections. Remember the child I mentioned who was bitten by a dog and became afraid of buses as a result? It's these subconscious and sometimes illogical connections that can give us the most trouble as we move into adulthood.

I remember a client whose brother had died suddenly when she was in her early teens. She related the psychological issues she was experiencing as a result of this traumatic experience and told me how she had been seeing different therapists for some time to help her change the way she thought and acted. When she came to see me, she had started a process of psychotherapy called Inner Child Therapy. This involves becoming familiar with the child that resides within you and helping that child through a process of nurturing. My client had experienced some relief with previous therapists but was frustrated by a feeling of being stuck: the therapy she'd had was no longer moving her forward. I was curious about her belief that her problems stemmed from losing her brother so we began the process of examining her life before this incident. She started to describe an older brother whom she adored, but who would take risks and get them both into trouble. We began to see patterns in how she dealt with her brother's demands and antics and how they related to her existing problems with challenging people. My client eventually realised that the child within whom she needed to nurture was actually much younger than she had previously thought. It was this child that she needed to give support to, rather than dealing with her brother's passing. Finally, her therapy began to move forward and she gained understanding and control.

All the experiences a child has, along with the illogical associations they make with those experiences, help to create the subconscious beliefs that will mould the behaviour of that child right through their teens and into adulthood. Most behaviours are set between birth and the age of seven, or thereabouts. That's not to say these behaviours are with us for good. They can be challenged and changed but if we want the change to be lasting, we need to be able to recognise them for what they are. Often, an event in adulthood will intensify a behaviour that was mainly lying dormant. When this happens, it's because the logical mind has, for the most part, disproved the behaviour over time. However, a major life event can counteract all of this logical conditioning so that the original belief and its associated behaviour resurfaces.

There are schools of thought that look at the differences between the sexes and compare them with our prehistoric behaviour. Husband and wife co-authors, Allan and Barbara Pease, have covered this subject well in their books. They postulate that the differences between men and women can be related back to the hunter-gatherer lifestyle. Back then, the men mainly did the hunting and protecting: roles that required a very single-minded and logical approach. Women, on the other hand, mostly did the gathering and family rearing: roles that required multi-tasking and the formation of strong social bonds. The authors looked at how women depend more on the half of their brain that provides social skills, whereas men depend more on the half of their brain that provides logic and problem solving. In one of their books, there is a simple test that helps you to see whether you have a more 'male' or a more 'female' brain. I was amused and unsurprised to discover that my brain is more 'male' than that of some men! I love problem solving and logic, but struggle to engage with more modern social interaction and gossip. I am therefore unable to name any celebrities and refuse to watch soap operas!

Freud also looked at the relationships between children and their parents, often putting quite sexual meanings on the interactions between them. Meanwhile, the Swiss psychiatrist and psychotherapist Carl Gustav Jung had more archetypal theories regarding these interactions, believing that the mother and father persona is remembered in a collective subconscious that we all possess, irrespective of culture. I suspect that the behaviour we expect children to exhibit in relation to their parents comes from the way our parents related to us as children, as well as the way we view ourselves in relation to the rest of the world.

The generalisation that girls are like their mothers and boys are like their fathers often rings true, and it is commonly said that if you want to know what your husband or wife will be like in old age, you should look at how their respective father or mother behaves. This is because girls usually subconsciously pattern the behaviour of their mothers and boys pattern their fathers. This is not always the case, though. I have seen many examples of girls exhibiting behavioural traits similar to their fathers, especially when there is no male sibling for the father to relate to. Equally, boys may develop their mother's patterns of behaviour.

I had a client who went from one abusive relationship to the next. Often, women who get involved with these types of men come from families where the mother has been abused. This behaviour is learned from the mother and her interactions with men. However, in this client's case it was her mum who was abusive towards her father, with whom my client had built a strong bond. Despite her obvious femininity, she was also a 'tomboy' and struggled to relate to her mother. So it wasn't surprising that she went on to emulate her father.

As discussed earlier, how we behave can have a profound impact on our children and can mould their adult personalities and their relationships. We can pass messages on to our offspring that we are totally unaware of. The overly cautious parent might constantly remind their children to 'be careful', telling them not to jump/run/climb as they might hurt themselves, etc. This is often because the parent in question has little confidence in their own ability, and views certain aspects of the world as extremely scary. However, what the child hears is often a subtler message. What they might hear is: 'I don't trust you'/'I have no confidence in your abilities' and therefore, 'you are not a capable person'. The end result of this is a child, eventually becoming an adult, who lacks confidence and is scared of their own shadow. This can also lead to trust related problems such as Obsessive Compulsive Disorder. A child who has this sort of upbringing may also grow into an adult who has to constantly prove how capable they are to everyone - a people pleaser!

There are no set rules for how we turn out, although there are some general guidelines that can give us an indicator. We generally follow patterns of behaviour, and these can pass through generations. Recognising and breaking these patterns not only revolutionises our lives but the lives of generations after us. I take great satisfaction from working with people to resolve issues that they share with their parents, knowing that we are not only changing their life, we are also potentially providing their children with a happier, more balanced life too.

Dealing with Stress and Depression

As discussed previously, our current lifestyle is markedly different from the one that our distant ancestors had. Our stresses and worries are different and so is the way we deal with them. Prehistoric man suffered more physical stresses than we do. His concerns lay with physical safety, food and warmth. If prehistoric man was hungry, he had to go in search of food. If he was cold, he needed to find firewood or create a shelter. As food and shelter have become more accessible to us and our ways of obtaining them fall under tighter social constraints, our concerns have moved away from the need to take direct action and towards obtaining something much less tangible, i.e. money or a relationship that increases security. This is clear when you look at the process of going to work in order to obtain money to buy food. Sitting in an office as a means to fill an empty belly is very far removed from what our ancestors needed to do to solve the same problem. Of course, there are some extreme examples, where people believe themselves to be so desperate that they take direct action to feed and shelter themselves. However for the most part, our route to providing our most basic needs has become much more convoluted and complex.

The upshot of this is that often, in order to solve our problems, we need to 'think' as much as we need to 'do'. This in itself is not a problem. We are by nature problem solvers and it is our ability to think that has helped our brains to evolve to the stage they are

at now. However, there is still part of us that retains our forebears'
need for action: to be able to do. *sobrecargados.*

When we become loaded down with problems and concerns, we
have a tendency to dwell on them, to get lost in our own thoughts.
We examine options, explore ideas and more often than not, end
up going round in circles. We get so involved in thinking that we
stop doing. Physical activity is good for us in all sorts of ways. It
keeps our bodies trim, our circulation healthy, and it produces
all sorts of hormones and enzymes that keep us, including our
brains, in balance. When we get loaded down with worry, we
often slow down physically too, which is exactly the opposite of
what we need to do in order to keep our brains balanced and
working efficiently. This is why it is routinely accepted that people
suffering with depression should exercise. As well as keeping us
physiologically balanced, it fools our brain into believing we are
taking positive action towards improving our situation, which in
turn makes us feel better. When we feel better, we are more able
and equipped to deal with our problems.

The other change that tends to happen during depressive
episodes is that we limit our own choices. The world becomes a
place of black and white, where there is the choice between only
two available options, neither of which is acceptable to us. We get
so obsessed with those two choices that we become blinkered to
all other options and can see no way out of our situation.

I have seen many middle-aged women who've come to me
because their relationship has failed. They have spent their lives
being wives and mothers and when their relationship collapses,
they have no idea how to deal with it. They simply don't know
what else to be! Strangely, they come to me at the point where
either they are considering returning to their partners or have
met someone new who is not quite right them but fills the void.
The challenge for these women is that they see only two options:
to be in an unsatisfying relationship or lose their identity as a wife
and carer. To these women, neither option is acceptable. The first

means returning to a situation that has already proved itself to be unsafe, the second is terrifying as to be without a partner is to lose their own identity and not know who they are or what their purpose is. One of my first jobs when dealing with these women is to help them see that they have other options. When they begin to explore what it is to be a little selfish, to enjoy things for themselves, their depression and fear lifts and they begin to function again.

When people suffering from depression can identify what remains polarised for them (i.e. the two bleak options they may feel are their only options), they can be encouraged to consider other concepts that may have not occurred to them. This technique, in conjunction with exercise, can be highly effective at moving people towards positive change. Thinking our way out of problems is all very well, but sometimes we need to do as well.

A useful way to create options and change is to have clear goals. We all need to strive. Striving is part of human nature and not having anything to strive for, i.e. not having goals in your life, can lead to depression. Having goals gives our lives structure and brings us a sense of purpose. If you have a clear goal that seems too big, it is possible to break that goal down into a series of smaller goals, each of which will take you one step further towards your ultimate aim. As you create smaller goals, you also create choices that give you greater flexibility and more options. Many people are familiar with the concept of SMART goals. Created primarily for business challenges, SMART goals were introduced in a paper by George T Doran in the 1981 publication, *Management Review*. However, the SMART concept works just as well for the setting of our personal goals. In fact, in order for our personal goals to succeed they must be SMART.

SMART stands for -

- **Specific** - we need to know exactly what we are aiming for in order to maintain focus.

- **Measurable** - we need to be able to measure our success, otherwise, how do we know when we achieve it?
- **Attainable** - Our goals need to be within our reach. If your overall goal seems unachievable, breaking it down into smaller goals that are recognisably achievable is a useful technique.
- **Relevant** - A relevant goal is easier to envisage. Is it worthwhile to you at this time in your life?

- **Time Bound** - It's important to set yourself a timescale to stop yourself from being distracted and to give you an end point to work towards.

Sometimes it's worth looking at the challenges in your life to see if they are SMART. If they don't fit into the SMART criteria, it's unlikely that you will ever achieve them, so make sure you are spending your time and energy wisely.

A client of mine was once struggling to understand just how in control of her life she actually was. She felt like all her choices had been taken away from her and that she was being forced down routes that she didn't want to take. Towards the end of the counselling session, I asked her what she was having for dinner. Puzzled, she replied that she was having fish pie. Then I asked her how many choices she would make from that point until she ate her meal. She struggled to name more than one or two. Then I pointed out the times she would make a choice: whether she would wear her coat or carry it, whether she would choose to stop at a junction or drive into oncoming traffic, whether she would add onions to her pie, etc. She had a huge number of choices to make. We could have identified hundreds, thousands even. This exercise showed my client just how in charge of her life she actually was, and how many times she had the ability to choose. It inspired her to continue to look for choices, to increase her options and therefore increase her opportunity for success.

This client had a major goal: to have fish pie for dinner. It was specific as she knew what she wanted, it was measurable as she knew that when she had eaten it, she would have achieved her goal, and it was attainable as she had the means to make the pie, i.e. the ingredients and cooking tools. It was relevant due to the fact that it would further her wellbeing and it was time bound as she knew that she needed to achieve all of this by teatime. There were many routes she could have taken to reach her goal and each route contained lots of smaller SMART goals. It's amazing what we can achieve if we open our minds to the variety of choices that are available to us.

Summary

In this chapter we:

- ✓ Discovered how evolution works and how human evolution affects modern day behaviour.

- ✓ Learned how we respond to certain 'anchored' sensory experiences.

- ✓ Looked at how prehistoric children stayed safe and how we still retain those behaviours.

- ✓ Explored feelings of abandonment and how this is used to teach social boundaries that can affect our adult relationships.

- ✓ Discovered how young children create beliefs from their relationships with their carers.

- ✓ Learned about how children develop logic, and how this affects the way they think.

- ✓ Discovered how the illogical beliefs created in early childhood can stay with us in adulthood.

- ✓ Looked at theories surrounding how men and women are different and how we respond to our parents, as well as the subconscious messages they give out.

- ✔ Considered how our ability to gain food and shelter differs from our hunter-gatherer ancestors
- ✔ Looked at how thinking rather than doing can lead to depression, and how depression causes us to limit our own choices and options.
- ✔ Learnt how to create sensible goals and how these can help to give our lives structure, purpose and meaning.

Specific
messurable
Attainable
Relevant
Time bound → time limited

CHAPTER 3
How Relationships Work

they are driven to do
↳ determined

Games

tal y como esta

There are times when people don't want to admit to having options because, on a deeper level, they are driven to continue with the relationship or behaviour as it stands. These are the people who play the 'yes but' game. In 1964, Eric Berne, a Canadian-born psychotherapist, published a book called The Games People Play. This book described how people act and react within relationships, creating 'games' that they relive over and over again. The book became an international bestseller and made Berne famous for his work in what became known as Transactional Analysis. In the 'yes but' game, people will reveal their unhappiness over a situation but ignore suggestions as to how they might change it. This happens because although they consciously recognise how the situation is detrimental to them, on some subconscious level it fulfils a deep-seated need within them. In other words, solving the problem creates more fear for them than living with the problem itself.

When people are closed to the choices available to them, they sometimes deal with their situation by normalising it to themselves. This is particularly apparent when talking to people who are in an abusive relationship – here the 'yes but' game comes into its own. 'Yes but' becomes an opportunity for someone to try to explain irrational thinking or behaviour, either their own or someone else's (and even both sometimes). People pleasers play the 'yes but' game all the time. This is because it is much easier to give in to unreasonable demands than to say no. Rather than risk displeasing someone, they will come up with any and all manner of excuses as to why they can't withdraw from the situations they find themselves in. Someone who has normalised their situation can be particularly difficult to help, as they will argue in loops to try and justify their behaviour or situation, although on some level they will be desperate to acknowledge how dysfunctional it has become.

I recognise an element of 'yes but' within myself, from when I was in the damaging relationship mentioned in the first chapter. On one hand I knew I was woefully unhappy and unsafe, on the other, my desperate need to be the perfect partner for this person held me within the relationship. I would listen to the advice of friends, relatives and even counsellors but I struggled to overcome my subconscious drives. Only when the situation became urgently unsafe for me could I justify walking away from someone who 'needed' me. My physical safety was so threatened that it became primary in my need for Ultimate Safety and Comfort. Even though I had walked away in order to remain physically safe, the temptation to keep returning to my partner was immense. It was only when I gained the real insight that my need to be perfect was holding me within the relationship that I was finally able to walk away for good. I came to understand that I had been fighting myself all along.

People in abusive relationships are often considered to be weak by outsiders looking in at their situation. In reality, it can take tremendous effort to continue to try to please an abuser despite the abuse experienced. The real challenge is to say no, either by standing up to the abuser or by walking away. The latter option is usually the safest but it requires the people pleaser to leave their abuser to manage his or her own life, which can be far more challenging psychologically to the pleaser than continuing to live with the abuse.

Anyone wishing to fully understand behaviours that are repeated within relationships would do well to gain a basic understanding of Transactional Analysis, not just to understand the role of their companion/associate but also to form a deeper understanding of their own emotional drivers. The concept of game playing will become especially important in later chapters when we deal with relationships and people pleasing.

What Drives Us

As I've already mentioned, I don't believe in the selfless act. This is because when we look at how we have developed over the millennia, it's clear that we have evolved to respond to physical, mental or emotional stimuli. A sunflower will follow the sun as it moves through the sky. This is to allow the plant maximum sunlight to increase its energy levels. The flower has evolved to take advantage of a genetic mutation which allowed it to grow faster than its stationary counterparts. Equally, the Russian physiologist Ivan Pavlov saw that dogs responded to a ringing bell by salivating when they had been trained to associate this noise with food. Our survival is paramount to us, as described earlier in relation to Ultimate Safety and Comfort. Everything we do is designed to keep us alive and well.

Let's look at this concept in terms of some of our personal drivers. Often, we seek comfort in food. This is totally natural, bearing in mind that we have evolved to desire the nutrients most likely to ensure our survival. However, our modern lives are not as physically exhausting as our ancestors'. We may well come home from work tired but for many of us, the exhaustion is mental rather than physical. Our brains aren't that good at differentiating between physical and mental stress, and they have a tendency to treat them both the same. This means that we have the same desire for calories (and therefore energy rich foods) whether we are exhausted mentally or physically. In short, we expect the foods that bring us physical comfort to bring us mental comfort too (and remember, our taste buds are geared by evolution towards increasing our desire for the foods that bring us physical comfort).

When we comfort eat, we are seeking mental comfort: the gastric equivalent of having a hug. The problem is, the more gastric hugs we have, the more calories we consume. This is OK if we then burn these excess calories off in a healthy and sustainable way. Problems arise when we become obsessed with the net result that these extra calories can have on our bodies. For some people, the idea of becoming overweight brings its own mental discomfort in the form of self-loathing and guilt. This then brings about a feeling of mental discomfort and distress, suggesting to the brain that the person is no longer safe. The way the brain handles this is to provide the body with energy that will help it to survive. This comes in the form of...you've guessed it...calories. This comfort eating becomes a vicious cycle of self-loathing and reward that for some people becomes totally out of control.

The best way to handle this is to find new, healthy and more sustainable ways to give ourselves a 'hug'. One technique that I have found particularly helpful for clients who have issues with comfort eating utilises both the concept of reward, and appeals to the child within us. This is particularly effective as it is our inner child that often creates our extremes of emotion but it also responds most effectively to forms of behaviour modification. I suggest to my clients that they decide on an item or experience of value to them. This needs to be something reasonably within their financial grasp but something that they would not usually treat themselves to. Often, this is a new item of clothing, a technological gadget or a spa day/ makeover. This becomes the client's goal. I encourage the client to keep this goal in mind by imagining themselves enjoying their reward, writing down their thoughts as though they are experiencing it in the present, and creating a scrapbook (or similar) containing images of their reward, which they can look at whenever they want food. These are NLP techniques that help to retrain the brain to go towards the reward and away from comfort eating. The goal has to be earned by periods of 'good behaviour', which is signified by stars on a calendar or something similar. Good behaviour may be sticking to a healthy diet or refraining from snacking. If the client divides their day into three parts, they may have a star for each period of good behaviour. We decide together how many stars the client will need in order to earn their reward. This system takes the emphasis off food as a form of reward and punishment. As the stars become the reward, the diet stops being a punishment. The reward (hug) is available several times a day in the form of stars and the client finishes up with a larger reward at the end of the exercise instead of a larger waistline! Incidentally, this way of managing comfort eating also fits nicely into the concept of SMART goals.

So how does this idea of rewards or hugs fit in with relationships? Every time we share something with another person, we have either a positive, neutral or negative experience. In Transactional Analysis (TA), these are called 'strokes'. The example Eric Berne uses describes the strokes given during a chance encounter in the street. If you see someone as you walk down the street, you may smile at them. This is a stroke. If they smile back, they are giving you a stroke. And naturally, we like the strokes we receive to be equal to the strokes we give. When someone you know walks past, you might say good morning and expect them to return the gesture. If they ignore you, you might feel a little put out that your stroke hasn't been returned. The concept of the stroke is the same as the concept of rewarding certain behaviours.

In relationships, we work with the concept of reward and punishment all the time. The rewards and punishments are usually not physical in nature, although they can be. They are usually connected to our desire to be liked, loved, valued, respected, appreciated or feared, and our need to be perceived as powerful, nice, strong, ruthless or distant, etc. Each time we communicate with another living being, we are, on the deepest level, attempting to ensure our own survival. That sounds like a rather dramatic statement, doesn't it? What we are looking for in our communications with others is the best possible outcome for us, even though on the surface, it might seem as though we end up with something less desirable. Remember earlier when we looked at the concept of Ultimate safety and Comfort? In our communications with others, we seek to satisfy our subconscious desires before our conscious ones.

That's OK when all of our conscious and subconscious desires are congruent: we can be comfortable and at peace with our choices. What happens though if they are incongruent? In this situation, we can be left with emotional upheaval as our different parts fight for supremacy in the battle for Ultimate Safety and Comfort. As it's difficult for both people in any communication to have Ultimate Safety and Comfort unless their needs and desires are totally synchronous on every level, we end up compensating in order to finish up with a compromise that works on some level for both parties. Eric Byrne referred to the manipulation of the communication process in order to find that compromise as a game. He postulated that all of our communications are games of a sort, and he recognised that we will often play the same game over and over again when faced with the same individual or personality type, even though the subject matter of the communication may differ. He spent some time describing the types of common games in his aforementioned book 'The Games People Play'.

Emotional States

In his work, Byrne described three major states of behaviour: the child, the parent and the adult. He postulated that when we are born, we are free of experiences. As a result, we are only able to see the world in a positive light. In this state, we can be a 'happy' child, one that sees the world through curiosity and excitement. However, once we start to experience the world, we discover what it means to be unhappy and to experience hurt, fear and anger, which in turn creates a 'damaged' child.

As our development continues, we become aware of the world in terms of other people and their experiences and behaviours. Generally, the people who have the most profound effect on us at this stage are our parents, because we spend most of our time with them. We observe their behavioural patterns and absorb them into our own.

Have you ever been entertained by a toddler stamping their feet and making demands as though they are your parent? When we observe this parental behaviour, we see two different styles. There is the 'nurturing' parent: one who is supporting, encouraging and allows the child to explore and grow and the 'critical' parent: the one who says 'you can't do that' or 'don't be stupid'. It is perfectly natural that as adults we exhibit both of these behavioural types at some point: no person is perfect. Finally, as development continues, the child discovers the purity of logical thought, where decisions can be made free from emotional input. This becomes the 'adult' self.

Within the theory of Transactional Analysis, we all have the following personality types: the healthy child, the damaged child, the adult, the nurturing parent and the critical parent. In a well-balanced person, the main state will be that of the adult, with the person sometimes drifting into the healthy child or nurturing parent. However, very few people reach this state of balance. Most will spend at least some of their time in the damaged child or critical parent state too. People suffering a greater imbalance may spend more of their time in the parent or child state than in the other two. We have all met people who seem particularly childlike or who have a very parental attitude. This stems from the messages that they were given in childhood and how they chose to respond to them in order to survive. It may be that they have adopted those behaviours for themselves, or they have developed coping mechanisms, which they deploy whenever they are confronted with those behaviours. See figure 4 on page 68.

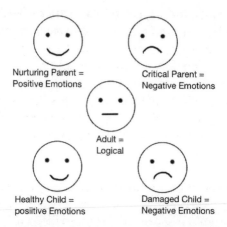

Figure 4. The five transactional states

When we communicate with others, we can switch from state to state with surprising speed. We can change state in response to our beliefs about the state of the other person, even though we may have misread their message or intentions. See figure 5 below.

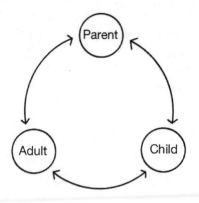

Figure 5. The transitions between transactional states

Consider an argument between two adults. It may be that the argument started when one person asked a question in the adult state but the other person responded to what they perceived to be a question posed in a parental state. For example, person A might say: 'I can't eat this dinner.' This may be because they have a dental problem or are feeling ill. However, person B may see this as a parental criticism of the meal they prepared. This might throw person B into their damaged child state. They might respond by saying: 'I hate you, you're never satisfied.' The argument may continue in this pattern if person A is then thrown into their critical parent state and says 'don't be so stupid', or they might respond as a damaged child themselves, declaring, 'you're always moaning at me'.

Some people find it easier to be in one state more often than the others. It could be that they find it easier to play the role of child over and above the roles of parent or adult or it may be that for them, the parent state is strongest. It could also be that they find the emotional states of child or parent easier to be in than the logical adult state.

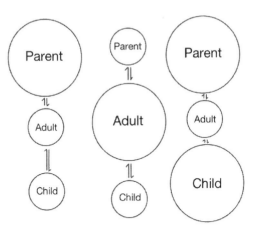

Figure 6. One state may be more prominent in some people than the others

This switching of roles becomes very important in relationships. Often, although the subject matter of arguments may change, the response pattern will remain the same. This is called a 'game', although often it is far from entertaining. What we subconsciously see in people becomes very important when exploring how we interact with them. Simply the way someone looks can subconsciously remind us of someone with whom we have previously developed a game pattern, causing us to attempt to recreate the same pattern with the new person. Just to complicate things further, we are often drawn to people who remind us of those we have had relationships with before. This makes the likelihood of repeating the same games all over again even more probable.

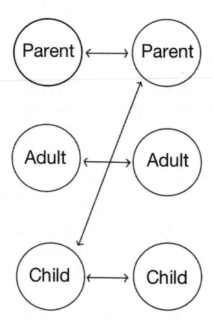

Figure 7. How two people can communicate within different transactional states

Why Play Games?

A common term within game playing is co-dependency. This basically means that both people involved in the game are benefiting from playing it. This seems very odd at first. Why would someone partake in something that is potentially very unpleasant? One of the most well known examples that Byrne gave of co-dependency is that of the Alcoholic and the Rescuer. The alcoholic drinks both because of its immediate self-medicating effect on their emotional issues and because they subconsciously want to be placed in the position of the child, to be scolded by the parental rescuer. If the alcoholic reforms, not only will they not be able to self-medicate, they will also not receive the scolding they require, possibly because it reaffirms their self beliefs or allows them the pleasure of seeking the approval of the rescuer. In turn, if the alcoholic reforms, the rescuer is denied the opportunity to be the 'helper' and also the 'superior' person within the relationship. Therefore, it is in the interests of both parties for the alcoholic to continue to drink and for the rescuer to rescue.

People pleasers often play the game of 'look how hard I've tried'. I can relate to this within my own previous relationships and in my desire to be 'perfect'. Equally, abusers often play 'see what you've made me do' to justify their actions. We will explore both of these games in later chapters but for now, the important message is that if you can recognise that you are involved in regular game playing, either within one relationship or in many, as hard as it is to accept, on some level you are benefitting from that game. This can be hard to face up to and even harder to decipher but in order to create change within yourself and subsequently in how other people treat you, you need to understand why you do what you do.

Having the deeper self-knowledge that comes from recognising our part in such games enables us to increase our perception of the world and ourselves. The greater the perception you have, the easier it is to make more constructive decisions for yourself. One of the world's most debated questions is: 'what is love?' From a psychological point of view, my definition of love, or any other relationship for that matter, is the degree to which you get your conscious and subconscious needs fulfilled. This doesn't really differ from our other relationships, which also require the same level of fulfilment. What changes is our expectation within that relationship. You probably wouldn't expect a work colleague or the guy you buy the morning paper from to 'love' you. Your wants and needs from those people are less complex; there are fewer of them. Love only affects those relationships that we enter into in order to meet our deeper conscious and subconscious needs.

Consider if you will a tower of boxes that extends both above and below the ground. Within each box is a want or need. Above ground are all the boxes that relate to our conscious needs and below ground are all the needs that our subconscious demands. In our relationships with more general associates, we require that only a few of those boxes are filled. In more important relationships, we require a much larger percentage of the boxes to be filled. Remember how we require fulfilment in mind, body and spirit in order to reach our Ultimate Safety and Comfort? Those requirements become our boxes, some of which are obvious to us and some of which are much less so. The filling of these boxes is what binds us in a relationship and our subconscious needs bind us more firmly than our conscious ones, just as our mental 'basement' provides the foundations for our 'house'. This means that unless we get to know our subconscious needs, we can be bound to people without really understanding why and often against our 'conscious' better judgement! See the diagram below.

Notice that in our subconscious set of boxes, there are wants and beliefs that can act both for our benefit and our detriment. It doesn't matter how many conscious boxes are ticked, if a subconscious box is empty, it will leave us feeling unfulfilled. Conversely, if all of our subconscious boxes are ticked, this will override the need to fill all of our conscious boxes. In other words, we find ourselves with people who logically we know are bad for us but who we cannot withdraw from.

So what happens when our partner cannot satisfy an important need? This can happen as we change and grow and our needs change too. Often people find a substitute to fill that box, i.e. they have an affair or develop a crush on someone else. In reality, the substitute doesn't have the means to fill all the required boxes either but a need that has not been filled for some time can become very powerful and cause us to seek fulfilment from someone who is actually rather inappropriate as a partner.

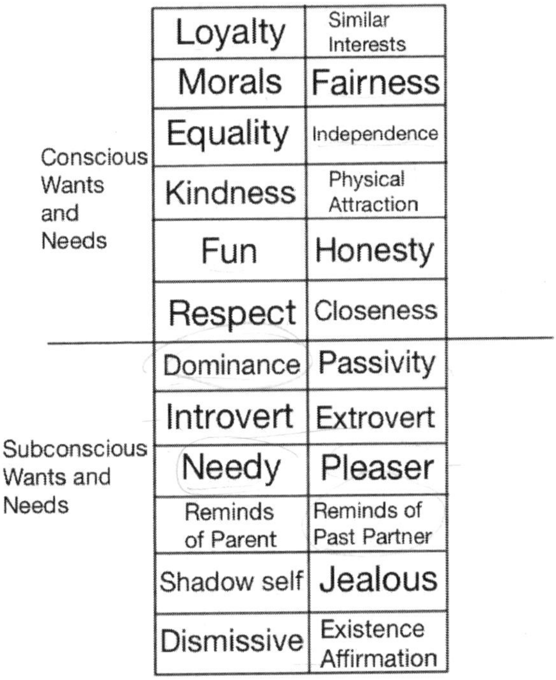

Conscious Wants and Needs	Loyalty	Similar Interests
	Morals	Fairness
	Equality	Independence
	Kindness	Physical Attraction
	Fun	Honesty
	Respect	Closeness
Subconscious Wants and Needs	Dominance	Passivity
	Introvert	Extrovert
	Needy	Pleaser
	Reminds of Parent	Reminds of Past Partner
	Shadow self	Jealous
	Dismissive	Existence Affirmation

Figure 8. Some potential wants and needs

In order to make sound judgements regarding what sort of relationships are good for us, we need to really understand our subconscious beliefs. Once we understand them and bring them into our conscious thoughts, we can start to challenge them and ensure that only those that are genuinely useful to us drive us. In other words, we need to move those boxes from the subconscious into the conscious, where we can apply logic to their appropriateness.

crutch - F -> mulete

The Shadow Self

even though

On the subject of relationships, a popular saying is that 'opposites attract'. Why is this and exactly what does it mean? Often within a couple, there will be one partner who is dominant and one who is passive, one who is tidy and one who is messy, one who likes life to be organised and one who is carefree. Yet as much as these two opposites are in a relationship based on 'love', each one will be irritated by the failings of the other. In other words, by the very aspect that makes their partner opposite to them.

I have seen this occur in many of my relationships. You may remember how I was drawn to any behaviour that helped me to be the 'perfect' partner. This often meant being with someone who had many emotional or intellectual needs, which meant that I could attempt to solve all of their problems. I didn't realise that I was drawn to needy people simply because I had a subconscious desire to be needed! However, this was often the cause of the relationship's downfall, because I chose people who had needs that were so demanding of me (either by seeing me as an emotional crutch or basically wanting me to run their life for them) that this began to threaten my own Ultimate Safety and Comfort. It was only at this point that I could remove myself from the relationship. In this way, you can really see how opposites might attract! ▷ mulete

When I was training with Tom Barber and Sandra Westland, they taught me an exercise that really helped me to understand why opposites attract. This might be interesting for you as well. Take a few moments to think of a person that you have a real intense dislike for, one who you perhaps know only loosely. Now try to isolate what it is that you really dislike about them. When I did this exercise, I realised I disliked a particular person whom I saw as being especially needy of the people around her. I intensely disliked neediness, yet I was attracted to men who were needy. Why would this be?

The answer lies, of course, within my own subconscious beliefs. A large part of the concept of perfection within a relationship for me meant being self-reliant: not 'taking' from another person. The idea of having to ask someone for help was very difficult. For me, to see another woman be so needy was difficult to bear, as the thought of being needy myself was abhorrent. So why would I choose a partner with this exact behavioural trait? A well-balanced person is capable of balance in a relationship. They can give and take, be dominant and passive, messy and tidy in turns. We all crave this sense of completeness, of being whole. However, our subconscious beliefs about ourselves seldom allow us to develop completeness. We possess certain traits, such as being introverted or negative (or extroverted and positive) and find people with the opposite of those traits hard to understand. We are unable to absorb those opposite traits within ourselves and yet we need them to feel whole so we might seek out a partner who possesses them. The side of us that we can't bear to hold inside is called our shadow self. The problem with having our partner act as our shadow self is that it doesn't allow us to grow in completeness ourselves. When one person in a couple does start to seek growth and change in themselves, often the other person cannot or will not seek growth and change in the same way and the relationship becomes mismatched. If this happens, inevitably there will be a battle where one partner struggles to hold onto their new identity whilst the other tries to hold onto the status quo.

What we actually need to do is come to terms with our own shadow self. Part of becoming balanced and 'whole' is to understand that moving outside of the comfort zone of our beliefs is good for us. It's good for the introvert to learn that it is safe to enjoy lots of company, just as it's valuable for the very needy person to become more self-sufficient. Conversely, it's helpful for the extrovert to be comfortable in their own company and for the self-reliant person to discover what it is to accept help from someone else.

One of the most significant events for me when it came to creating my own change occurred when I was discussing a problem with my mother. She wanted to help me with something but I didn't want to let her. At one point, she said to me in a frustrated tone: 'You know, when you constantly deny any help from anyone, you are denying them the pleasure of being able to help you.' I simply hadn't seen the situation in this light, but of course it made sense. If I got my sense of purpose from helping others, why shouldn't anyone else feel the same way? It made me realise that accepting help could sometimes be a good thing and it paved the way for me to start to change and become more whole. As I mentioned earlier, my relationships are more balanced now. Over time, I have learned not to try to be perfect. These days, I expect the people with whom I have relationships to accept me for who I am and not to make unreasonable demands on my time, energy or emotions.

It's hard for someone to find balance when they have a partner that conveniently plays the part of their shadow self. That partner will do almost anything to ensure that the relationship is maintained because they have their shadow self in you and need you to complete them. Imagine a seesaw with a person sitting at each end. Those people are in opposing positions but balance one another out.

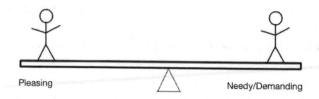

Figure 9. Finding the balance between your partner or shadow self

Many games are played between couples (either in an intimate relationship or otherwise) that are using each other as their shadow selves. Whilst either will find the other difficult to be with, losing their shadow self and becoming less complete is worse. The games that play out between them in order to maintain the relationship in a manner that is bearable can be very complex and stressful.

In accepting and embracing the traits of our shadow selves, we become more balanced, closer to the pivot point on the seesaw. When this happens, we find less need for our shadow selves and the relationship starts to break down naturally. Have you ever heard anyone say: *'I've grown but they haven't'?* As people grow or change, so do their wants and needs in a relationship. In a healthy relationship, people can grow together and adapt to each other's growth. My first challenge to people pleasers is to allow other people to help them. This is something that is surprisingly difficult for them to bear.

Understanding your wants and needs within a relationship can be very liberating. At Hope Level Therapy, I help people do this, either as individuals or as couples. It helps to understand how the role of the shadow self impacts the relationship and how needs change as life situations change. Often, it's just about communication. It really is surprising how couples that have been together for years can struggle to communicate their most basic needs and the role of a therapist can become one of an interpreter. I once saw a couple at the brink of splitting up because the husband had retired and being together all the time was causing them all kinds of problems. I got the husband talking about how he felt (losing his role of breadwinner) and the wife talking about how she felt (that her territory was being encroached on). In just one hour, they were seeing themselves and each other completely differently and left my office hand in hand.

Not all relationships can be helped so easily. If the couple really is mismatched, the best thing that can be done is to help them find an amicable way to part. Again, this is about good communication. There is often a great deal of blame, guilt and hurt when a couple splits up and the only way through this is to help both parties understand themselves so that they can make sense of what they are feeling.

Summary

In this chapter we:

- ✔ Understood the nature of 'games' within a relationship, and how people 'normalise' behaviour.

- ✔ Learned why people pleasers find it hard to say no.

- ✔ Discovered that it is our subconscious beliefs that drives us, and how our drivers relate to our relationship with food.

- ✔ Looked at social strokes as a concept and how this links to reward and punishment.

- ✔ Explored the three states of behaviour: adult, child and parent - as recognised within Transactional Analysis - and how they interact both within us as individuals and within relationships.

- ✔ Considered co-dependent behaviour in relation to games, in particular to people pleasing.

- ✔ Discovered how the concept of love relates to fulfilment within a relationship on a conscious and subconscious level.

- ✔ Understood what our shadow self is and how sometimes we choose partners with the same characteristics of our shadow self.

- ✔ Learned that embracing the shadow side of our personality allows us to become more balanced and enjoy more balanced relationships.

CHAPTER 4
People Pleasing and
Why it Hurts

What is a People Pleaser?

So what exactly is people pleasing? The truth is, if you are a people pleaser, then you probably know exactly what one is, although you may also be reading this book because a friend or loved one is people pleasing right now and simply won't admit to it. People pleasers are, simply put, individuals who just can't say no. This can be with family, friends or colleagues and it can take over and even destroy someone's life.

In an earlier chapter, I discussed the concept of the selfless act and how people are driven to make the decisions they make. There are a great many things that motivate us. These motivations are based on what we consider - consciously and subconsciously - will give us the most satisfying type of reward. For some people, a reward on an emotional level could be an acknowledgement of their power, an expression of gratitude or recognition. At its most basic level, this may even mean that their very existence has been acknowledged, both on a physical and on an existential level. This can have a profound effect on someone, even though they may be totally unaware of their subconscious drive to be acknowledged.

Imagine living in a world where you cannot be seen, heard or felt. Only your most extreme attempts to communicate are recognised and then they are often misinterpreted or dismissed. Imagine how frustrated and isolated you would be. It would be pretty awful to have to take more and more extreme action in order to be communicated with and it would leave you wondering if you even existed. The vast majority of us are very lucky not to experience this kind of isolation but even though we can and do communicate reasonably well on a day-to-day basis, there is a tiny, subconscious part of all of us that fears this. Remember the naughty spot? That place where children go to learn the error of their non-conformist ways? Well, we never really get over this fear of abandonment and it can become part of our subconscious drivers as adults. As this drive is subconscious, it can be far more powerful than any conscious, logical decision that we might make.

So how does this fit in with people pleasing exactly? Remember the previous chapter when I discussed strokes? Well, a stroke for some people could be an acknowledgement that they have worth or value. The problem with this is that the worth or value that the people pleaser recognises is not always the same as it is for the person they are attempting to please. The important word here is attempting. People pleasers rarely get what they think they want. If they did, they wouldn't be people pleasers! Effectively, people pleasing is another type of game. The two people playing the game are both compliant but the person doing the pleasing usually has a distorted sense of responsibility within the game, feeling that their companion's happiness depends on them. Sometimes the game is productive and both people feel satisfied but more often than not, the game is the opposite, leaving one or both players confused and hurt.

People pleasing is about repeatedly conforming to another person's wishes, even though this choice causes the people pleaser in question some form of personal discomfort. We all do things that we don't want to do from time to time. That is a natural and normal part of life – it's the give and take that forms healthy relationships. Without it, human society would quickly pull itself apart. However, when sacrificing our own wants and needs for the sake of the wants and needs of others becomes a regular occurrence, we can move into a downward spiral. In terms of Ultimate Safety and Comfort, the overwhelming subconscious driver is satisfied but achieving this may mean sacrificing more logical wants and needs, such as physical safety.

The Unspoken Contract

Let's have a look at the people pleasing process in more detail. When a people pleaser chooses to please, they are seeking a specific response from the person they are attempting to gratify. The game is productive when they get the result they want and it is unproductive when they don't, either because they get something different or because they get nothing at all. Imagine that you have gone to the market to buy an apple. You carry out your side of the bargain by providing the fruit vendor with money. How would you feel if, instead of giving you an apple, they gave you an orange? Or even worse still, they took your money but didn't give you anything at all? You'd probably feel pretty fed up that the vendor hadn't given you want you wanted and you might spend even more money trying to get it from them or someone else. People pleasing is a lot like this.

The essence of good, healthy relationships is clear communication. Unfortunately, in the people pleasing game, this doesn't happen very often. I like to think of the people pleaser's attempt to get a reward as an unspoken contract between themselves and the person they are trying to please. I will work your shift, give you control of the remote, let you decide how I dress, etc., if you make me feel wanted, appreciated and recognise that I exist. Does that sound familiar? The problem is that this is an unspoken contract. The people pleaser is effectively creating a bargain that the other person may be unaware of or fail to understand.

If you compare the fruit market scenario with real life, the money becomes the people pleasing behaviour and the fruit becomes the reward. You either get the type of reward/fruit that you wanted or you don't. The difference is that when you buy fruit, you consciously know what you want out of the contract. People pleasers often aren't aware of what motivates them. The first step in managing your people pleasing behaviour is therefore to take a long hard look at your situation and figure out your underlying needs.

As I mentioned earlier, my people pleasing was linked to being the perfect partner and more specifically, to doing things for people to a very high standard, so that my efforts stood out over and above anyone else's. In relationships, this meant being the best cook, the most efficient administrator, the most diligent organiser, etc., which meant that I would always be better than anyone else who might threaten my role. In my childhood, this often meant being compliant, selfless or even invisible. I would become whatever people needed me to be. It took me a while to learn this lesson and it kept coming up in surprising places.

In my rather disastrous relationship, I sought to please by being the perfect administrator and manager of my partner's business. I made sure I was there for him whenever he needed me, which turned out to be pretty much 24/7. This was unsustainable for me because no matter what I did, it was never good enough. I simply wasn't getting the recognition that I craved, i.e. an acknowledgment that I was perfect. For my partner to do this, he would have had to admit that I was doing enough, something that his own narcissistic personality couldn't allow.

After we split, I resolved to never be with another needy man and found myself with a guy who was exactly the opposite. I was pretty smug about having learned my lesson. The new guy was incredibly independent, to the point that he was determined not to have a full-time meaningful relationship, mainly due to traumas he had suffered as a child. At first I enjoyed this newfound freedom, but slowly my people pleasing behaviour crept back. As I started to crave more substance and quality in the relationship, I became perfect at being the closet girlfriend, which satisfied what he wanted. I was the kind of girlfriend who didn't complain when he failed to get in contact for days at a time, one who would put up with his inconsistent behaviour in order to keep him happy. The odd thing was, the more I worked at it, the more distant he became. One day, something snapped in me and I realised that yet again I was involved in a relationship where I was giving up what I wanted, i.e. a loving, equal relationship that had generosity on both sides, to be with a man who was making me jump through hoops and would never be satisfied. It wasn't until I really understood the depth of my problem and its many guises that I could really start to enjoy the level of honesty that I have in my present relationships.

These days I can laugh at my drivers and ignore them but before I understood myself as I do now, they caused me a lot of misery. Part of the reason for this was that I sought out relationships with people who were virtually impossible to please. The people I was forming relationships with had their own problems and neuroses that prevented them from enjoying healthy relationships too. This is fairly common with serial people pleasers. The important thing is not to look at the actual pleasing acts themselves but to explore the patterns of behaviour that cause you to do things that you don't want to do. Look for the games and extrapolate on their meaning (as discussed earlier) to find out what really makes you tick.

So effectively, a people pleaser can experience one of three things in their people pleasing. They might get the reward they seek (which suits both parties perfectly) but more likely they will either get something different to what they wanted or nothing at all.

This takes us back to the concept of the unspoken contract. The people pleaser doesn't necessarily know exactly what they want but believes the person they are pleasing implicitly does and is able to provide it. This is not a conscious belief and the people pleaser generally has no idea that they are doing this. The net result is one of extreme frustration to the people pleaser. They do what they think is necessary to gain a reward, only the one they most often get isn't the one they were looking for. Their sense of fairness tells them they should be grateful but they are left with a feeling of emptiness due to a reduced sense of worth which their lack of any meaningful reward leaves them with.

An example of this would be the worker who offers to come into the office over the weekend for an urgent assignment. They knuckle down and do the work very well. On Monday, their boss instructs his or her PA to tell the employee that they can take an extra three days as holiday to compensate. The boss has been more than fair, rewarding the hard work with one and a half times the rate of time that the employee has sacrificed. However, the worker feels used and hurt. What they really wanted was to be told personally by the boss that they had worth. The employee is aware that they have been treated fairly but they do not feel valued. In fact, by giving back more time than was due, the boss may even be giving the message that the worker isn't needed as much as they might have thought. This is a very confusing scenario for the people pleaser.

The Gift

The other experience a people pleaser might encounter within the contract situation is to not receive anything at all. Basically, the person they are attempting to please sees the situation very differently to them. Whatever the pleaser is offering is not part of a contract (as the pleaser believes). Instead, it is actually perceived by the person they are pleasing as a gift.

Back at the fruit market, someone speaking gibberish has just walked up and given you money for no reason. Despite being thrilled you are confused by their motives and cannot understand why they would do such a thing. However, you pocket the money, certain that if they offer you it again, you are going to keep on taking it. After all, it would be silly to give up such a good thing. You have no idea that the gibberish they are speaking actually means: 'please can I buy an apple from you?' This is what people pleasers are actually doing when they don't make their contract clear. This is a common experience, as most people pleasers generally get some kind of satisfaction from the situation, even if the result is only a re-enforcement of their beliefs about their own self worth. The reward is actually to be recognised by others as someone who goes the extra mile. Some would refer to these types of people pleasers as martyrs; individuals who revel in telling other people how hard done by they are by their spouse, partner, parent, child, co-worker, etc (playing the game of 'look how hard I try'). The reward comes from the misguided belief by the pleaser that their often Herculean attempts reveal that they are a special person.

People pleasers struggle with the rejection of their pleasing attempts because they cannot act on what they learn. Often the people pleaser is fully aware that their behaviour will not get them the reward they crave but they carry on regardless due to their subconscious drivers. This can be a repeating pattern, either within the same relationship or in several. Often, they are aware of what they are doing but are loathe to stop doing it. Why is this? Once again, the answer lies in our ancestral heritage.

Competition and Territories

Anyone familiar with the natural world knows that survival can only take place if each organism has its own territory. All living creatures need basic functions to live. In simple organisms, this is the ability to consume nutrients and water and to be free of their own excreted by-products. Plants compete for sunlight and nutrients, as any gardener who has neighbour with a coniferous tree too close to them will know. The tree will take most of the available water and nutrients from the surrounding soil as well as creating shade, which will stop the plants beneath it from growing. The home brewer will be familiar with the concept that the yeast growing in a barrel of beer or wine will utilise all available nutrients and produce it's by-product in the form of alcohol. This will continue to the point where the alcohol it excretes prevents further growth and the yeast becomes inactive. This is why beers and wines have limits to how much alcohol they can contain without fortification.

experiments

When we apply this to higher forms of life, things get more complicated. Each species and each individual animal even, needs its own space in which to thrive. Evolution is basically when a life form spontaneously and randomly undergoes a mutation in its genetic material that creates a change in its shape or behaviour that enables it to survive better than other life forms of the same type.

This provides the life form with a competitive advantage that may enable it to be more successful at reproduction. If during reproduction this change in genetics is passed onto the progeny, a whole new group of life forms is created. When a creature has evolved to live in a very specific environment, we call this its niche. Charles Darwin showed examples of this in his study of finches in the Galápagos Islands. Each sub species of finch had evolved a slightly different-shaped beak, which enabled it to eat a specific type of fruit, nut or insect. Many species of finch could live happily within the same environment because their niche, i.e. what food they needed, was different.

As well as inter-species competition there is intra-species competition. Organisms from within the same species will compete for the same niche and the winner gets the most optimal one available. Animals from within the same species will fight for food, water, homes and mates. Sometimes this fight may be a show of their physical attributes, much like some form of natural beauty contest. The bird of paradise exhibits its plumage, whereas the bower bird creates a beautiful nest site. More often than not, physical strength is used as a measure of success, with animals creating complex fighting rituals to identify the stronger animal whilst minimising the physical risk to the competitors. Some fights do go to the death but as this defeats the overall aim of propagation through reproduction, most animals will avoid this. The strongest animals have the best niches, which will be the most comfortable and spacious and will contain the highest quality food, water and mates. These animals will have the ability to fight for and defend their niche. Weaker animals have to survive in progressively sub-optimal niches, where comfort,

marge

space, food and mates are more scarce or of a poorer quality. Life on the fringe can be tough so weaker animals are less successful in propagating their genetic material through reproduction.

Once upon a time, the human race also had to fight amongst themselves to ascertain who was the strongest. These days, our fight to find a niche of our own to occupy has become the most complex ever. We attempt to strive towards improving our environment in everything we do. This can be witnessed through the careers we choose, where we decide to live and via those we pick to socialise and identify with. Society no longer allows us to take up a club and beat our way to supremacy. Our day-to-day struggle to find and keep our niche has become much more sophisticated. However, we do all need a niche of our own within which to be physically and mentally safe. Every transactional game between people is an example of how we jostle to find a way to co-exist with others, much like the Galapagos finches. We strive to find a relationship that gives us a niche. However, this is not always logical because our need for a niche occurs often at a more basic, instinctive and subconscious level.

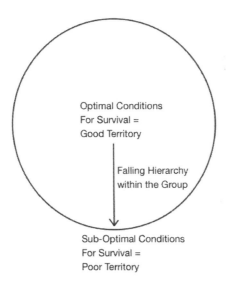

Figure 10. Hierarchy within a group defines the quality of territory for the individual within the group

You may be familiar with the concept of personal space - that invisible area around you where certain people are welcome and others are not. This is a type of territory: a place that we are calling our own. When someone invades your personal space it creates a feeling of discomfort. Depending on the situation, it might even trigger a fight or flight response, forcing you to either remove yourself from the situation or physically remove the invading person. How do you decide who is allowed into your personal space and who isn't? Do you make a logical, conscious decision every time you interact? Probably not. The decision is almost always made on a gut level. For example, if you have a feeling that someone is creepy, it can be hard to define exactly what it is that is creepy about them. We define our personal space in such a way that as someone moves towards us, our discomfort gradually increases. This can be imagined a bit like the layers in an onion. Some people are allowed in our outer layers, others are encouraged to come much further in.

Oddly enough, exactly the same thing happens with our mental and emotional space, although not many people realise this. Our need for personal space on a mental and emotional level is, if anything, more important than our physical space. It's as though we have evolved to the point where the way we fight for our niche no longer involves physical battles but rather psychological ones - games. We let people into our mental and emotional onion every time we acquiesce to a request that makes us uncomfortable in some way. The closer to the centre of the onion a request becomes, the more painful it is for us. Imagine that request as a boxer attacking you. If he is too far away, his blows cannot reach you. The closer he gets, the more pain he can inflict. (See figure 11 on the next page) √ /əkwiˈɛs/ ⇒ ceder

Compare this now with the battle that people pleasers have to fight in order to say no. It can be comparatively easy to say no to a simple request or to a stranger. However, the more important the person or request becomes to the pleaser on a subconscious level, the harder it gets to say no. When people pleasers find themselves in that awful position where the person or request touches them very deeply, it can be virtually impossible for them to say no and break away, no matter how much they know that this is the logical option. The same person or type of person can continually make requests of a people pleaser and that can make the people pleaser appear to be completely at their mercy. The pleaser knows exactly what they are doing and will even try to rationalise their behaviour in order to lessen the difficulty of explaining why they won't stop. Their own personal niche or territory has become so small that it has become non-existent. The people pleaser is actually doing something totally normal in the context of territorial behaviour - giving up a better territory in order to preserve personal safety. They are like the animals that live on the fringe of the niche where life is hard, the ones that don't attempt to fight stronger animals for a better one.

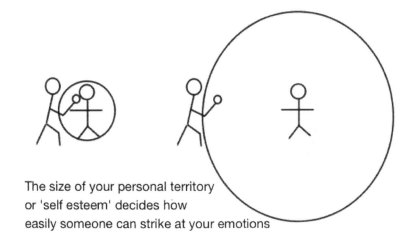

The size of your personal territory
or 'self esteem' decides how
easily someone can strike at your emotions

Figure 11. The amount of self esteem we have can affect how we respond to emotional attack

I have seen examples of 'pleasing cascades' at work. These occur when a people pleaser (let's call them A) gets stuck between pleasing two other people with opposing needs. When one of these two people is a people pleaser themselves (B), A might

sometr

choose to satisfy C, the most dominant person, knowing that B will understand and accept their dilemma. If B submits to A, C is effectively being pleased at the top of the cascade, and A is being pleased in the middle. B remains at the bottom, having sacrificed their own needs to both A and C.

People have differing success at make demands
of us, depending on our relationship with them

Figure 12. How the nature of a relationship dictates our vulnerability to emotional attack by that person

However, if B stands up to A, A has to be responsible for their choice regarding whether they satisfy B or C. They have to decide where they stand in the hierarchy, and who stands above and below them. In an ideal world, they would consider themselves as valuable as both B and C, and the pleasing relationship would break down. In reality, the pleaser becomes very introverted, unhappy and depressed, as their choices are significantly reduced.

This sort of situation may occur for example, where a person is trapped between pleasing a partner and pleasing a parent. If the parent and the partner are opposed, the pleaser faces an enormous dilemma as to who they should be loyal to.

I believe that our mental and emotional personal space is very closely linked with our self-esteem. The more self-esteem you have, the better you are at defending your territory from those who would make demands from you, or, in other words, the more comfortable you are with saying no. Conversely, the less able you are to defend your territory, the lower your self-esteem can become, and this can be an ever-decreasing circle.

Dealing with Insults

A friend of mine shared a quote from the Idealist Facebook page on his personal page. This went: *"In order for you to insult me, first I have to value your opinion."* This reminded me of a very valuable lesson in dealing with insults, which I learned many years ago from an extraordinarily talented relationship counsellor called Denise Knowles. I think that it's well worth sharing here.

One of the easiest ways to hurt someone is through name-calling and personal criticism. Being called a 'stupid cow' or 'thick' or 'fat' or any other insult, is not only incredibly demoralising, it's also very inflammatory and can lead to retaliation, making an argument many times worse. Insults are a very effective way of controlling someone. They are a way of showing and maintaining power and control. This is very hierarchical behaviour, as it is basically saying: *"I'm better, stronger and more aggressive than you."*

By responding to insults, what you are doing is effectively taking ownership of them. Even if you are disagreeing, in order to disagree you have to be showing the insult some consideration. Effectively, in doing so, you are validating the insult. This means that you are giving the person who is insulting you empowerment and validation - you are letting them inside your territory. For example, if someone calls you a "stupid bitch", even if you respond by saying *"no, I'm not"*, you have had to consider whether or not you are a stupid bitch before giving your response.

A better way to answer would be to say, "you think I'm a stupid bitch". Just that, nothing more. In responding this way, you are making it clear that whilst you have heard the insult, you aren't in any way taking ownership of it. In effect, the insult stays with the person making it and will not encroach on your territory. You are not giving them any power over you.

I once had an experience where someone tried to bully me through argument. I quietly stood my ground and every time my opinion or ability was called in to doubt, I simply smiled. Eventually, the person involved showed his frustration by insulting me, which I simply ignored. Whilst I haven't had a particularly good relationship with that person since, I haven't experienced any of the bullying that I have seen them do to other people. They knew that I simply wouldn't allow them to feel powerful at my expense.

Going back to the original quote - *"In order for you to insult me, first I have to value your opinion"* - you can only give value to someone's opinion by responding to what they say. In dealing with insults by making it clear that their opinion stops with them, you are telling them that their opinion is worthless.

Summary

In this chapter we:

- ✔ Looked at what drives the people pleaser in their behaviour, in relation to their ultimate safety and comfort.

- ✔ Learned how good communication is important in relationships and how not stating what you want and expect clearly can lead to an unsatisfactory outcome.

- ✔ Discovered how important it is for the people pleaser to be able to identify what drives their behaviour.

- ✔ Saw how people pleasers are not always clear in what they expect from others, which leads to not receiving the reward they want or not receiving a reward at all.

- Learned the importance of territory and having a space of your own.

- Discovered that we need mental and emotional space of our own, just as we need personal space.

- Explored how people pleasers give up their territory to more dominant characters.

- Discovered that pleasing relationships can be very complex, involving more than two people.

- Discovered how to handle insults by not allowing them in to your territory.

CHAPTER 5
Options, Saying 'No' and the Road to Recovery

Empathy

In the previous chapter, we discussed the three situations that people pleasers can find themselves in. If you remember, we were at the fruit market. We saw that there can be three results to asking for an apple. Either the customer gets their apple, they get an orange instead, or they don't get anything at all. In terms of people pleasing, this can mean getting the reward you want, getting a reward you didn't want or not getting a reward at all. The latter two outcomes are the ones that cause the most problems.

People pleasers usually share two things in common. One is that they have an excellent ability to empathise with other people's wants and needs, the other is that they have a very strong sense of justice.

People pleasers are usually very, very good at empathy and seeing situations from different perspectives. They have quite a broad view of the world and often have a good understanding of what motivates others. This works against them because they can understand exactly why someone wants them to do something and can measure it against their own needs. It also helps them in their games of 'yes but' as it provides them with excellent reasons why they should continue to please. Unfortunately, the low self-esteem that comes with people pleasing can mean that they undervalue their own worth on some level, so the other person's needs always appear greater than their own.

Many people pleasers go into sales jobs because the intuitive skills that allow them to understand what other people want and need also helps them to empathise with their clients. The problem is that they also find it difficult to ask for the top price for their product because their people pleasing encourages them to put their customers' best interests in front of their own. Unless they genuinely believe in the benefits that their product will bring to the purchaser and that the product is worth the asking price, they will struggle to sell. Their body language will give them away and will create doubt in the mind of the purchaser.

Although low self-esteem allows people pleasers to prioritise others over themselves, the logical part of their brain has a pretty good idea that the situation lacks balance and that they give more than they receive. This is a factor in creating the frustration and depression that people pleasers tend to experience. They see that by continuously making unreasonable demands of them, other people are not measuring their worth as equal to everyone else's. They are hurt and confused by this as there is no logical reason why this should be the case. Remember the boxes of wants and needs? The subconscious box that drives people pleasing behaviour is dominant, but the people pleaser can still experience all of the conscious boxes, for example the one that demand respect.

If you imagine this enhanced view of the world and understanding of others in terms of a Venn diagram, where the box contains the whole of the universe, the people pleaser fails to know everything in the universe but they do have an expanded awareness compared to someone with less empathy. (See figure 13 on the next page)

Unfortunately, the individuals that people pleasers attempt to satisfy are, if anything, less well equipped than most in terms of understanding and empathy. This is because people pleasers often choose companions who have a very narrow view of the world, which is based purely upon their own wants and needs. When this is highlighted in the Venn diagram, the difference

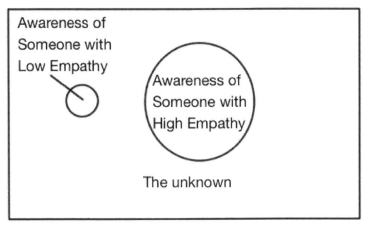

Figure 13. The difference in empathic awareness between a pleaser and someone with greater self absorption

between the two character types becomes obvious. When the people pleaser attempts to satisfy someone, they expect to be within the awareness parameters of that person. Have you ever heard the expression: 'You can't fit a quart into a pint pot'? The people pleaser's sense of justice created by their logical half knows that they should not give up so much of themselves for another person.

People pleasers are often very angry with the people that they are pleasing. This is partly because they can't understand why that person is acting so unfairly and partly because they are afraid that they genuinely might only be worth the value they have assigned to them. They are fearful of giving up so much of themselves in order to fit inside the world view of the person they are trying to please. When viewed by an observer, the situation looks even more unbalanced and leaves the observer wondering why the pleaser does so much for someone they so clearly hate. Hate is a strong word but it is an emotional one. It is possible for a people pleaser to both love and hate the person they are pleasing in equal measure. The very reasons why the people pleaser loves the person they are pleasing are the same reasons why they can also hate them. Their subconscious needs are met and their conscious needs are unfulfilled. What the people pleaser both loves and hates is the ability of the other person to make unreasonable demands of them. They hate this because they feel used but they love it because they can continue to attempt to please. They have found their shadow self!

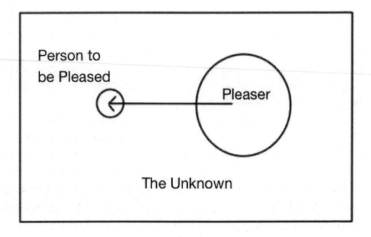

Leads to

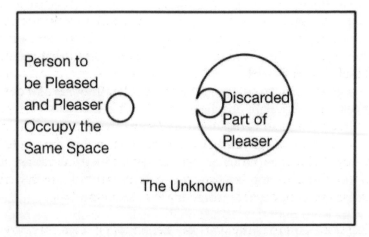

Figure 14 & 15. Living within the universal construct of someone with less awareness can mean having to leave a part of your self behind

Options

The picture I'm painting of the people pleaser is highly complex, to say the least. For them, it isn't as simple as just saying no. In fact, the thought of saying this can actually make them feel physically ill as the distress caused is so great. So how do we go about helping the people pleaser? The first step is for them to understand the logic of the situation. Remember my earlier assertion that options are important? There are four basic options available to the people pleaser. Option one is to carry on pleasing but as you are still reading, it's fairly safe to assume that you can see the benefits of choosing a different route.

A second option is the one I call 'the God option', for want of a better name. This option allows people to carry on pleasing by enabling them to find a new source of comfort from their pleasing behaviour. The reason I call it the God option is simple. Many people who have a profound belief in a religion or spirituality choose this option as a way of dealing with their people pleasing. The idea is that they will sacrifice their needs to someone whose needs are greater in order to seek fulfilment from a higher entity, i.e. If I do this selfless act, I will secure my place in heaven/God will love me/I will atone for my sins/I will reach a higher plane. This often gives them the comfort they need to continue their behaviour, even though they recognise their discomfort within the behaviour itself. Their need to please is rewarded by their belief that their behaviour will be rewarded eventually, even though this would not be by the person that they have set out to please. For example, they may say, 'I will help that selfish and ungrateful person because God will send me to heaven.' I'm not talking here about working in soup kitchens or building wells in drought-ridden countries. I'm talking about handling the discomfort of caring for a relative who is demanding and spiteful, or a friend who never seems to try to help themselves.

The third option is the first real step in using logic that people pleasers can facilitate to help themselves. This option provides them with an opportunity to take real action towards making a change in their situation, and it is based on the concept of the unspoken contract. The people pleaser needs to create effective and well-communicated contracts with the person they are pleasing in order to give that person a chance of fulfilling the contract. This will also give the pleaser clear boundaries, which will help them to establish if their contract has been met.

Setting a clear contract is dependent on the people pleaser being able to improve their communication so that they can be sure that the individual it relates to has the opportunity to meet their side of the bargain. The easiest way to do this is to ask the other person to repeat back to you what you want from the bargain. For example, a people pleaser might say: 'If I agree to take your shift next week, you'll need to take one of mine before then.' Notice how the emphasis is on the person being pleased fulfilling their side of the bargain first. This is perfectly acceptable as they are asking you for the favour, so they need to commit to being trustworthy.

If the person is asking for a favour which they don't have a chance to reciprocate first, try to create some space before agreeing. This does two things. Firstly, it gives you a chance to see if they will keep their side of the bargain and secondly, it gives you some emotional space from the situation so that you can say no if necessary. For example, if someone asks to borrow money, say that you need time to check your account first in case some of your bills haven't been processed. The reason for creating a contract that needs to be met by the other person first is because people pleasers are often frustrated by individuals who fail to keep their promises. Just to be clear though, if demands are made that suggest that abuse will be a result of saying no, this is not a situation where creating contracts is a good idea. You can't and shouldn't attempt to set contracts with abusive people. In this case, seek professional help immediately, either from the police or victim support groups. We will deal with recognising abuse in the next chapter.

One of the reasons why it is important to verbalise unspoken contracts is that the people pleaser's sense of justice can be both satisfied and used to great effect. By saying the contract out loud and ensuring that the other person fully understands what is expected of them, the people pleaser can be sure that they are fully justified to suspend their help if the contract is broken. This level of justification cannot be underestimated. It allows the people pleaser to apply logic to the situation that is congruent to their subconscious needs. This congruency between the conscious and subconscious self enables change to occur on a much deeper and powerful level.

The final way of dealing with people pleasing behaviour also relies on consistency between logical conscious and subconscious behaviours, although it takes a little more practice. This method requires the people pleaser to learn from their games with the people that they please and to make pre-emptive decisions based on what they know to be fact. To put it in very simple terms - if you've never got the reaction you want before, you are unlikely to get it in the future so don't bother trying - just say no!

Accepting the Need for Change

As we've established, saying no can be incredibly hard for some people. So never underestimate how difficult this can be for someone in a very strong, people pleasing relationship. Don't forget, even though the relationship can be very painful and demoralising, the people-pleasing person is part of the game and so is benefitting from it in some way. Remember how in the chapter about games, I mentioned one called 'look how hard I tried'? Most people pleasers exhibit this martyr-style behaviour, whether they internalise it or express it externally to anyone who might be listening. Playing 'look how hard I tried' means repeatedly trying to please someone who, deep down, you know will never be grateful, simply to show how good you are for trying. Guess what, though...in order to feel balance and wholeness, you need to embrace your shadow self internally, not within an external relationship. That means being willing to accept that you aren't always expected to live up to being perfect and recognising that you just can't please some people. Imagine that... admitting to yourself that it's OK to fail!

As I said, saying no can be incredibly hard and will inevitably change the nature of the relationship between the people pleaser and the person they are trying to please. Sudden change can and probably will be too much for both parties and may result in so much strain that the people pleaser simply gives up trying. Imagine trying to get to the top of a flight of stairs. You can go up one step at a time or you can try leaping to the top in one go. If you leap, you'll definitely get to the top faster but you will also stand a much greater chance of falling. And, if you do fall, it will take you right back to the bottom and possibly leave you too damaged to try climbing the stairs again. It's far better to climb the stairs one at a time, taking it slowly. If you do stumble, you will only go back one step and will be able to attempt climbing it again. Saying no is a lot like this. It's far easier to say no to little things at first and slowly build yourself up, rather than change massively overnight and say no to everything. Remember the animals fighting over their territories? This is exactly the process you are going through. If you regain your territory a bit at a time, in manageable steps, you are far more likely to hold on to it. Of course, regaining your mental territory will change you – it will make you stronger, more confident and self-assured.

It may well be that the new you no longer fits into the relationship with the person you were pleasing. Is this such a surprise, though? Imagine the type of person who always wants other people to do things for them. Are these people balanced within themselves? Of course they aren't.

Imagine an old fashioned number line, one with a zero in the middle and negative numbers to the left and positive numbers to the right. When we have a relationship with our external shadow self, both parties are usually at equal distances from zero along the number line. For example, if you are a minus five, you tend to choose a partner who is a plus five. If you are a minus twenty, you will choose a plus twenty partner, and so on. As one person in a relationship gains balance, they move towards zero on the number line. Unless their partner is also capable of seeking balance, the number line becomes unstable. People who expect others to do things for them all of the time are not balanced people. This might be quite hard to accept but when people pleasers meet balanced people, they are not drawn to each other. That's because balanced people don't feel comfortable around someone who wants to wait on them and people pleasers don't feel comfortable around someone who is happy to help, as this makes them feel like they are being criticised for not coping.

Let's face it, someone who wants people to attend on their every need is not a good person to be in a relationship with in the first place. Balanced people can recognise this and will avoid those people completely. This is a very important concept to understand. You cannot change other people - that's up to them. You can only change yourself. If you can't bear being with someone as they are, don't try to change them. This will only hurt you in the long run. The best thing you can do (for both of you) is to find someone who is a better match for you, and accept it when they find a better match for them. It's hard to accept when the person you were trying to please meets someone new. This can seem like a rejection. Often, this will lead the people pleaser to feel as though they have failed, as the person they were trying to please seems to be doing things for their new partner that they would never have done for them. If this happens, remember the number line. Either they have met someone who doesn't balance them, in which case the relationship will fail, or, more probably, they have met someone who does balance them on the number line, so they will feel the need to impress them in order to secure the relationship. This new person is desirable to your ex partner because both your ex and their new partner are far behind you on the road to growth, self-discovery and contentment!

People pleasers will begin to find change and balance when they are able to recognise when the something they've been asked to do (or the something they have found themselves offering to do unprompted) makes them feel uncomfortable on some level. That recognition of self is the first step towards developing healthy relationships. It's at this stage that you have to be able to challenge yourself and your motives. You need to question why you feel the need to something that you know is not right for you on some level.

A client of mine was so proud to tell me in one session how she had refused a relative who had asked to borrow money from her. The relative had even said it was for a child in order to increase the emotional pressure on my client. Although she felt incredibly guilty, my client was able to see the situation for what it was and say no. She knew consciously that it was in her nature to try and please and was able to logically recognise and banish this feeling, knowing that the relative had already wasted money that week on alcohol and that the money would never be returned. My client was able to see that her need for the money was greater than her relative's.

As I said in an earlier chapter, we all need to be able to give and take, but there must be balance. If a situation is not right for you, remove yourself from it right at the start, whilst it's still in the outer layers of your mental territory. If someone cannot respect your right to say no, they are probably not a good person for you to enter into any kind of relationship with.

A good way to prepare yourself for saying no is to create two lists for yourself. In the first list, write down all the aspects of a relationship that are important to you. Don't just include personality traits, put down financial, geographical and any other factors that might affect your willingness to be involved with someone. In the second list, do exactly the same thing for all the things you don't want in a relationship. You can make these two lists for all your types of relationships if you want to, from intimate partners to work colleagues. It might seem strange to you that I've included things like financial or geographical circumstances but consider how would you handle a situation with a friend who asked you to lend them money, especially if you couldn't afford it or had doubts as to whether it would be paid back. It's helpful to think about what your response would be in advance, so that when you are put on the spot and your subconscious beliefs start to kick in, you have already got your answer and will have made peace with yourself as to how you came to that decision.

This technique is particularly useful in choosing intimate partners because there's nothing the people pleaser likes more than to play the role of rescuer. In other words, people who are in some way damaged are actually more attractive to a people pleaser than someone who is balanced. This is simply because if a person isn't damaged, there is much less for the people pleaser to do for them, which in turn means less opportunities for the pleaser to attempt to get the reward they yearn for. The damage doesn't have to be obvious. It could manifest as shyness, social awkwardness, alcohol or drug addiction, an inability to fend/clean/prepare meals for oneself, or a previous failed relationship. People pleasers are drawn to those who display these traits, even though the person may seem incredibly strong in other ways. For example, they may be successful in work, wealthy, physically attractive or highly articulate and intelligent. On the surface, the person that the people pleaser is attracted to may even appear to be highly independent but the subconscious part of the people pleaser's mind can hone in on weaknesses with remarkable accuracy. Is the person that you've just met able to make you feel sorry for them in some way, even though you don't know them and only have their version of their life events to make a judgement with? If so, beware! Feeling sorry is your emotional 'stuff', not theirs! YOU are reacting to them and only YOU can decide what reaction is healthy for you.

senhr lè'shinx

Summary

In this chapter we:

- ✔ Learned that people pleasers have good empathy and a good understanding of fairness, but low self worth.

- ✔ Learned that the people pleaser must give up a lot of themselves in order to exist within the expectations of the person they are trying to please.

- ✔ Discovered that this can lead to the people pleaser both loving and hating the person they are trying to please.

- ✔ Explored the options that are available to people pleasers and how to make these options work.

- ✔ Considered what it is like to embrace your shadow self internally and accept that you don't have to be perfect.

- ✔ Acknowledged that defending our territory changes us, and our relationships, for the better.

- ✔ Discovered that having a clear idea of what we want from a relationship at the start can prevent us from being tempted into a pleasing relationship.

- ✔ Learned what kind of person people pleasers are attracted to, and how to recognise them for what they are.

CHAPTER 6
When People Pleasers Meet Abusers

What is Abuse?

What happens when people-pleasing behaviour is very strong in someone and it is matched by equally strong demanding behaviour by the person they are in a relationship with? The answer is that the behaviour of the person they are trying to please all too often becomes abusive.

In order to understand this, we need to understand exactly what abuse is. A UK Home Office Government report published in 2013 defines abuse as: 'Any incident or pattern of incidents of controlling, coercive or threatening behaviour, violence or abuse between those aged 16 or over who are or have been intimate partners or family members regardless of gender or sexuality. This can encompass, but is not limited to, the following types of abuse:

- Psychological
- Physical
- Sexual
- Financial
- Emotional

The report defines controlling behaviour as: 'a range of acts designed to make a person subordinate and/or dependent by isolating them from sources of support, exploiting their resources and capacities for personal gain, depriving them of the means needed for independence, resistance and escape and regulating

Wind you up — mocking

their everyday behaviour.'

Meanwhile, coercive behaviour is: 'an act or a pattern of acts of assault, threats, humiliation and intimidation or other abuse that is used to harm, punish, or frighten their victim.'

The national UK charity Women's Aid gives the following signs of domestic violence on their website:

burlarse

Destructive criticism and verbal abuse: Shouting/mocking/ accusing/name calling/verbally threatening.

reputationado

Pressure tactics: Sulking, threatening to withhold money, disconnect the telephone, take the car away, commit suicide, take the children away, report you to welfare agencies unless you comply with their demands regarding bringing up the children, lying to your friends and family about you, telling you that you have no choice in any decisions.

Disrespect: Persistently putting you down in front of other people, not listening or responding when you talk, interrupting your telephone calls, taking money from your purse without asking, refusing to help with childcare or housework.

retener

Breaking trust: Lying to you, withholding information from you, being jealous, having other relationships, breaking promises and shared agreements.

Isolation: Monitoring or blocking your telephone calls, telling you where you can and cannot go, preventing you from seeing friends and relatives.

Harassment: Following you, checking up on you, opening your mail, repeatedly checking to see who has telephoned you, embarrassing you in public.

Threats: Making angry gestures, using physical size to intimidate, shouting you down, destroying your possessions, breaking things, punching walls, wielding a knife or a gun, threatening to kill or harm you and the children.

Sexual violence: Using force, threats or intimidation to make you perform sexual acts, having sex with you when you don't want to have sex, any degrading treatment based on your sexual orientation.

Physical violence: Punching, slapping, hitting, biting, pinching, kicking, pulling hair out, pushing, shoving, burning, strangling.

Denial: Saying the abuse doesn't happen, saying you caused the abusive behaviour, being publicly gentle and patient, crying and begging for forgiveness, saying it will never happen again.

These definitions often shock people who have been in an abusive relationship for years without acknowledging this because their partner hasn't been overtly physically violent. However, people pleasers all too often choose partners who are prone to abusive behaviour. The fault of abuse ALWAYS lies with the abuser. There is NO excuse for abusive behaviour in ANY relationship. However, in terms of game playing, the abuser may play the game of 'Look what you made me do', placing the blame on the people pleaser who believes that the fault is actually with them. When the game 'Look what you made me do' is combined with 'Look how hard I tried', you can see how the situation can spiral out of control.

Control

Abusers can be any age, gender, sexuality, size, culture or religion. They are not easy to spot and are often extremely charming to people outside of their control. It's easy to enter unknowingly into a relationship with an abuser, as they seem so capable and strong, not the kind of person who needs to make demands of someone else. However, something that all abusers have in common is a need to control the person that they are abusing. The abuser is so frightened of losing control over this person that they will

name-calling

subtil

often go to any lengths to maintain that level of power. This is why abuse is <u>insidious</u>. The level of control that the abuser needs to use is minimal at first. The person they are with is happy to meet their needs. The abuser will eventually become more and more <u>reliant</u> on the attention of their partner (although 'partner' can cover spouse, child, parent, sibling, friend or colleague) and cannot allow that person to share any energy with anyone else.

coupado

unide

Often, the abuser will seek to isolate their partner from friends and relatives and create a situation where they are <u>bound</u> to them, either financially or through children, property, etc. They will do this in order to have their partner all to themselves. This can include encouraging a partner to move in with them or to leave a job and be supported by them. Alternatively, they may develop illnesses or other situations, such as financial difficulty, to tie the partner to them emotionally and/or physically. As the partner begins to wear of this treatment, the abuser will begin to feel as though they are losing control so the cycle of abuse increases. The abuser may threaten to spread lies about their partner or to harm themselves. If the partner continues to show signs of independence, the cycle may turn to locking them in or out of the house and/or denying them access to a telephone or money. Eventually this can turn to physical violence.

renunuar

The abuser needs to keep their partner within the relationship as their shadow self - someone who will completely <u>relinquish</u> control to meet their need for ultimate control. They will do this by breaking down the self-esteem and confidence of the person that they are abusing via <u>name-calling</u>, criticism, etc. When the people pleaser is doing their best but all they find is complaint, rather than seeing this behaviour as unreasonable, they will assume that <u>the fault lies with them</u> so they will try even harder. Many people think that those who are in an abusive relationship must be weak. Actually, the opposite is true. It takes great <u>strength of character</u> to keep trying to please against all odds. However, this Herculean effort will always go unrewarded because abusers will never be satisfied.

the fault lies with him

Narcissistic Personality Disorder

Serious abusers often suffer symptoms of Narcissistic Personality Disorder (NPD), although I use the word 'suffer' with care because people with this disorder are usually completely unable to see any fault in themselves at all. The word narcissist comes from the Greek myth of Narcissus, who looked into a pool and fell in love with his own reflection. People with this disorder only see situations from their point of view and cannot recognise the needs of others at all. The UK National Health Service defines NPD as follows:

'A person with a narcissistic personality disorder swings between seeing themselves as special and fearing they are worthless. They may act as if they have an inflated sense of their own importance and show an intense need for other people to look up to them.'

Other symptoms include:

- ✔ Exaggerating their own achievements and abilities.
- ✔ Thinking they are entitled to be treated better than other people.
- ✔ Exploiting other people for their own personal gain.
- ✔ Lacking empathy for other people's weaknesses.
- ✔ Looking down on people they feel are 'beneath' them, while feeling deeply envious of people they see as being 'above' them.

There are many theories as to what causes NPD, but the one that makes the most sense to me is that someone suffering with it was exposed to extremes in parenting behaviour as a child, experiencing either one adoring parent and one contemptuous parent, or, alternatively, one parent showing either adoring or contemptuous behaviour in turns. This means the child will only experience situations where they are treated like the most important person on the planet or the most worthless one. Someone with NPD only knows these two extremes and very little in the middle. Of course, it's incredibly difficult to be the most worthless person on the planet. That is simply too painful to bear, so the person suffering from NPD only has the alternative of seeing themselves as the most important person in the world. The effect of this is that the NPD sufferer must charm people whom he sees as superior (those he cannot control) in order to gain their trust and gain equal or greater ranking. Anyone whom the NPD sufferer believes to be of a lower rank (or someone he can control) is simply not even a person as such. They become objectified and are seen as existing solely for the use of the NPD sufferer (well, in his eyes anyway).

The most important messages that I can give you about NPD sufferers are that a) they will NEVER be satisfied with your efforts. This is because to be satisfied with your efforts, they have to accept that you may be as good as them, which for them is impossible and b) even trained psychologists find these people notoriously difficult to treat, so you will NEVER cure them!

The best thing you can do in an unhappy relationship with an NPD sufferer is to leave. This seems very harsh but for the most part, an NPD sufferer will not even comprehend that he has a problem, much less seek help for it. You may have noticed that I am referring to the NPD sufferer as 'he'. This is because most sufferers are men. I suspect that this is because historically within society more emphasis has been put on making male children feel that they are special and yet must reach for higher goals, whereas girls are expected to meet the needs of their family by service rather than success. There are female NPD sufferers, however, just as there are male people pleasers.

The NPD sufferer is particularly adept at making the people pleaser feel worthless and a failure, and yet encouraging them to provide for his every need. The NPD sufferer has a tendency to objectify people and so feels no remorse for any abuse that they give. They see the pleaser as a part of their territory, much like a possession. They will justify abuse and maintain control over the pleaser by using the game 'Look what you made me do', placing blame for the situation away from themselves and onto the pleaser. When this happens, the situation can become very dangerous for both parties as the NPD sufferer also tends towards extremes of emotion and can easily lose control.

Getting Help

If you feel that this chapter relates to you, it is important that you seek the right kind of help. I have included some useful names, web addresses and phone numbers of UK support organisations on my website at www.hopeleveltherapy.com/emergency-help. Being in a situation where you cannot escape an abuser can feel very frightening and lonely, but these organisations know and understand what you are experiencing.

They will:

- ✔ Take you seriously
- ✔ Understand, even if there is no physical abuse
- ✔ Maintain your confidentiality
- ✔ Respect your wishes
- ✔ Help you to get out of the situation

If you are living with your abuser and want to leave, it is very important to *plan ahead*. Make sure you have easy access to important medication and personal documents, especially those that relate to your financial status and the place where you live. Try to keep a small amount of cash and possibly a phone on you at all times. Pack an emergency bag and store it in a safe place, such as with a friend you can trust. Make provisions for your children and plan to take them with you. Make sure you have the phone numbers of support groups handy. If you decide to leave, try to do so at a time when your partner is out of the house. If you feel as though you or your children are in immediate danger, dial 999. The police have a duty to protect you. Women's Aid provides a more comprehensive document outlining how to keep yourself safe and it's worth reading this through if you feel that you might find yourself in this situation. Leaving an abuser may not stop the abuse, but you are in a better position to remain safe if you have the right help and support.

Summary

In this chapter we:

- ✓ Learned what abuse is and how to recognise it.
- ✓ Understood that abuse is never the fault of the victim.
- ✓ Discovered that abusers seek control over their victims.
- ✓ Explored the symptoms of Narcissistic Personality Disorder and how people with this disorder can never be pleased.
- ✓ Looked at how difficult and potentially dangerous it can be for a people pleaser to attempt to stay in this type of relationship.
- ✓ Discussed where you can go for help and how to prepare to leave an abusive relationship.

CHAPTER 7
So, What's Stopping You?

Upsetting the Game

escape / get away

Whether you are struggling to stand up for yourself with a friend or work colleague, or in an abusive domestic relationship, if you could easily change the situation then you probably would. People pleasers really struggle to break away from the pleasing situations that they find themselves in. This is because they depend on other people to give them their sense of self worth. People with healthy self-esteem know that they are 'OK', without needing other people to reinforce that message. People pleasers, on the other hand, constantly need others to reassure them that this is the case.

In an abusive relationship, the abuser takes advantage of the pleaser's need for reassurance. Psychological abuse is now recognised in the UK as a criminal act, simply because the effect that it can have on the victim is so severe. In a co-dependent people pleasing relationship, where the pleaser and the needy person are mutually gaining, the needy person find ways of tugging on the emotional heartstrings of the pleaser. This could be by suggesting that some terrible event may befall them if the pleasing stops – 'I can't survive without you', or, worse: 'If you leave me, I will kill myself.' Alternatively, the needy person uses the situation to keep the pleaser in a constant state of low esteem by suggesting that they are, in some way, not good enough. Ironically, when discussing the pleaser with others, the needy person will often sing their praises. Don't be fooled by this. Remember that these needy people often strive to maintain a high place in the social hierarchy and they do this by showing how they have capable and effective people in their lives who are on a lower place in the social hierarchy.

Remember the number line? Imagine it as a seesaw with the pivot point at zero, the people pleaser sitting at -5 and the needy person sitting at +5 in terms of pleasing behaviour. The seesaw is in balance, i.e. the relationship is maintainable for both parties, with the people pleaser doing enough pleasing to balance the needy person's demands. However, inevitably, as life situations alter, one person in the relationship will start to change and the partnership will become unbalanced. Just as on a seesaw, if one person starts to move either closer to or further away from the central pivot point, things will start to tip. However, if both parties move the same amount but in opposing directions, the balance will remain.

Pleasing relationships will usually start with both parties being in moderate, opposing places on the seesaw: let's say -5 and +5. However, as the relationship progresses and the needy person feels more confident and in control, they will start to creep further away, maybe to a +5.5 or a +6, becoming more and more demanding. This causes an imbalance in the relationship, which the people pleaser tries to correct by trying harder to please, i.e. becoming a -5.5 or -6. This will continue until a point is reached where the people pleaser's need for Ultimate Safety and Comfort moves away from the need to please in order to build self-esteem and towards a need to maintain their self respect or personal safety. When this happens, the people pleaser starts to pull back, travelling back towards zero.

This does happen in healthy relationships too, but to a lesser extent. It's a fundamental part of human nature to be hierarchical and to assert yourself and your territory. However, in healthy relationships, there is give and take with the needy person moving towards zero to meet the people pleaser so that the balance remains. It is also possible in a healthy relationship for the people pleaser and the needy person to change places so that both people play the roles of people pleaser and needy person equally.

In pleasing relationships, as the people pleaser tries to pull back towards zero, the needy person moves further away in an attempt to maintain their advantage i.e. to +7 or higher. At this point, the people pleaser has a choice: either to break away from the relationship or to move further away from zero to -7 to regain the balance and status quo in the relationship. The needy person may then threaten the Ultimate Safety and Comfort of the people pleaser by either suggesting a threat to their own wellbeing or the wellbeing of the people pleaser. This may or may not be carried through. The threat of this may be enough to keep the people pleaser in the relationship. This kind of threat is abuse - the relationship has become abusive. In violent relationships, the people pleaser may well be at serious risk of physical, mental or emotional harm.

I have worked with people in all kinds of pleasing relationships: husbands and wives, parents and children, friends and colleagues. I have also worked with the clients of a women's refuge. They often experienced the extremes of being in a pleasing relationship. People give all kinds of reasons for staying in this type of toxic situation, but what it boils down to is the maintenance of the people pleaser's self-esteem through the value they feel others place on them. Without help or direction, the people pleaser will only leave the relationship if the threat caused by the needy person to their Ultimate Safety and Comfort outweighs the advantage of the pleasing behaviour and its effect on their sense of value.

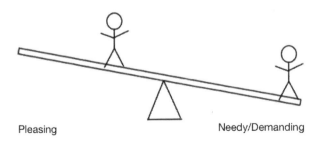

Pleasing   Needy/Demanding

Figure 16. How changing behaviour can affect the balance in a relationship

What do You Have to Lose?

In virtually every situation, the advantage of people pleasing behaviour is that the people pleaser gains their sense of value from the opinion of others. The people pleaser has no sense of value internally but is instead reliant on either the direct opinion of others or the subconscious drivers of being a 'good' person in their eyes. This is why it is perfectly possible for the people pleaser to have a strong dislike, or even feelings of hate, for the person they are pleasing and yet still carry on. They are worried what other people might think of them if they don't! The people pleaser has deep-seated beliefs about what it takes to be a 'good' person, which are usually created early in childhood. These beliefs are centred around the good opinion of others, usually a parent or another person of authority.

As we discussed in an earlier chapter, the good opinion of an important figure in early childhood has a huge impact on adult beliefs. In the people pleasing relationship, the demanding nature of the needy person triggers the deep-seated beliefs of the people pleaser around being a 'good' person, simply because the behaviour feels very familiar. This trigger is incredibly powerful and compelling, leaving the people pleaser driven to keep pleasing someone even though they have no idea why that person can exert such control over them. This can be highly frustrating for the people pleaser, leaving them feeling confused and out of control, which adds to their feelings of low self-esteem and value.

As people pleasing relationships become more toxic, the needy person can become much more demanding and unreasonable. Their behaviour can become exceptionally needy or offensive, far beyond the scope of normal social interaction. This change can be very subtle and insidious, with the people pleaser failing to recognise that this behaviour is not their responsibility. The people pleaser instead normalises it and blames themselves for it.

As the people pleaser takes responsibility for the behaviour of the person they are pleasing, they also feel the social pressure of this behaviour. They feel that if only they were 'better' in some way, the needy person would change. This thinking is encouraged by the needy person, as they will show occasional bursts of affectionate or even loving behaviour, which will lead the people pleaser to believe that they have the potential to change or be changed. This is a misguided belief. As discussed in the earlier chapters on pleasing and abuse, often the needy person does not have the emotional 'wiring' to be a part of a normal healthy relationship.

The result of the people pleaser taking responsibility for the bad behaviour exhibited by the needy person is that they feel shame and embarrassment for the situation that they find themselves in. Because the needy person can be remarkably charming to others who are outside of their control, the people pleaser often thinks that others won't believe them if they open up about the abuse they are suffering. Or they may even think that they will be blamed for it. This is why abuse often goes undiscovered and hidden for many years. It's also why the people pleaser struggles with the idea of the abuse becoming public via divorce, police action, etc.

It is important for the people pleaser to understand and accept that they are not responsible for the actions of the needy person. That person is wholly responsible for the circumstances that they find themselves in and it is perfectly reasonable for the people pleaser to stop helping them.

When I was in a very unhappy marriage, my sister did the single best thing for me that anyone could have done. As she and my parents spoke of my unhappiness, my parents said that they simply did not know how to help me. My sister pointed out that the one thing I really needed was reassurance that whatever I decided to do was OK. Of course, this was exactly how they felt but my sister knew instinctively that part of the reason why I didn't break away was because I knew how much my parents held the sanctity of marriage in high regard. However, in my people pleasing desire to be perfect, I had wrongly assumed that the marriage was so important that I had to stick with it at all costs. Hearing their affirmation that I needed to do what was right for me was exactly what I needed to be able to break free.

Often victims of abuse are surprised when they leave an abusive relationship and discover that they had the support of their peers all along. They often haven't realised that other people don't share the same overinflated view of their abuser that they have. In fact, often the abuser is considered to be weird and/or creepy by people looking in from the outside, and the victim is pitied.

From experience, I know that if you are a people pleaser, you may have struggled with some of the concepts described in chapter five about saying no. Now that you have a broader view of why you may be struggling, try rereading that chapter. Saying no is OK. Keeping yourself safe from harm is also OK. If you continue to struggle, consider talking to a therapist, counsellor or a support group such as Women's Aid. They can help you understand your motivations and help you to change.

Summary

In this chapter we:

- ✓ Learned what a person gains from a people pleaser, and how they maintain the relationship.

- ✓ Considered the seesaw analogy to see how change affects a co-dependent, people-pleasing relationship, and understand what a healthy relationship should look like.

- ✓ Realised that all sorts of people can be in a people pleasing relationship.

- ✓ Discovered that people pleasers need reassurance in order to break away, and that often other people see needy people for exactly what they are.

- ✔ Discovered that people pleasers are often surprised to discover that people outside of the relationship are 'on their side'.

physics

possession

symptoms

appropriate / appreciate

CONCLUSION:
Becoming Whole

So what has reading this book achieved for you? Hopefully, the following will have happened:

- ✔ You will have gained a better understanding of how the human mind works and what drives you.

- ✔ You will have learned how our hunter-gatherer ancestors have helped to shape our behaviour and how this fits in with our modern life.

- ✔ You will have considered the meaning of hierarchy in your relationships and where you place yourself within that hierarchy.

- ✔ You will have begun to understand the importance of upbringing and how it affects personality.

- ✔ You will have developed some understanding of relationships and how we interact with each other. You will have learned some theories on transactional analysis and on people pleasing, as well as gaining an understanding of abuse.

If you've read this book carefully, you'll understand that you shouldn't expect major change overnight. It's neither healthy nor desirable to make major emotional and behavioural changes all in one go, just in the same way that weight loss is more sustainable following a gentle change in the way you eat rather than crash diets. I hope I have encouraged you to be more interested in yourself and what makes you tick. Although we have spent some time looking at the behaviour of others, this is purely in relation to your own patterns of behaviour. Change needs to come from within.

So, what now? Hopefully, you will feel inspired to get to know yourself a little better. This could be through examining your behaviour or relationships and analysing the games you play and what causes you to be happy, sad, angry or frightened. A good way of doing this is with the help of a therapist or counsellor, someone who can be objective and help you see your story from new angles. A friend and loved one will not have the impartiality to play the role of a therapist. The games you share with them will impact on the quality of your explorations. I have an online therapy service where I give private, confidential, face to face therapy through Skype or similar services - www.hopeleveltherapy.com

A good therapist is not there to tell you what to do or how to do it; rather they will act as a guide and catalyst towards helping you to find your own route to change. Expect to partake in a number of sessions. Once you have experienced good therapy, you will find that there will be other times throughout your life when it beneficial to see a therapist. Our journey of change and experience continues through life. Just when you think you really understand a certain aspect of yourself, along comes another revelation that takes you deeper or in a different direction.

cauteloso

In the UK, people are still wary of receiving counselling or psychotherapy. We applaud our National Health Service and its ability to fix most physical ailments, and yet we fail to recognise the benefits of working on our mental health. When people express this reluctance to me, I liken it to breaking a leg. No one with a broken leg would expect to continue as normal without receiving help, and yet that's exactly what many people do when they are suffering from a mental or emotional trauma. If you spend money on your physical appearance, such as gym membership, expensive clothes, diet regimes, etc., then why not be prepared to spend a little on achieving a really healthy mental state? If you can't afford private therapy, consider asking if your chosen therapist does group sessions or see your doctor about NHS counselling. However, be wary of the fact that this service is under funded, the amount of counselling can be limited and there are usually waiting lists.

A good way of measuring change and getting yourself motivated for it is to use goal setting and a reward system, as I discussed earlier. Both of these are very practical methods of consciously creating a new way of being. It's also worth remembering how we anchor experiences to emotions. Practice changing your mood to a more positive or assertive one by listening to music or looking at or imagining scenes or images that match the mood you wish to be in. If possible, remember a time when you actually experienced the emotion you are trying to access. Recall every aspect. What were the colours, the sounds, the smells and the people and objects around you like? Take the time to recreate those feelings inside yourself and remember them. You can do this to motivate yourself to exercise, to work, to boost your confidence, to attend a difficult meeting or interview, or to find calmness or peace. I have downloadable relaxations on my website (www.hopeleveltherapy.com). Alternatively, the internet is full of other guided meditations to help you achieve different emotional states.

As with many therapists, I strongly advocate imagining yourself as the person you want to be. Write down what you are experiencing in present tense, as though you are that person, and spend a little time each day reading what you've written and relaxing with your eyes closed, imagining this to be your new reality. In order to reach a goal, you have to know, in your heart of hearts, that it is possible. Inside every submissive person, there is a calmly assertive person waiting to get out!

From this point on, the journey belongs to you. You can continue to allow yourself to put others before you or you can choose to understand what it is that you are looking for in that behaviour and find more productive, healthier ways to get what you need. Learn which of your wants and needs live in your subconscious and bring them out into the bright light of conscious thought, to be considered logically and satisfied in a way that is congruent for you.

I would love to say that I never people please anymore, but that would be a lie. I am continually learning about myself and noticing ways that I people please or seek 'strokes' from others. Where the difference lies is that these days, I spot when it's happening and I learn from it. I rarely get caught out the same way twice! So I leave you hoping that you also will enjoy seeing yourself and others in a new light, and that you will credit yourself with the qualities that you deserve and dismiss those that others have imposed on you. I hope that you will choose a better place for yourself on life's hierarchy and learn how to keep that place. Maybe you will start to see hierarchy operating in the relationships of others and how they react. You may even feel inspired to learn more about psychotherapies and how they can help you in your own development or allow you to help others in theirs. Maybe you'll even follow my footsteps and become a therapist yourself. Either way, I wish you all the success and growth you deserve.

WHAT NEXT...?

I'd love to hear from you!

If you have enjoyed reading this book and would like to know more about how I can help you, then visit my webpage, www.hopeleveltherapy.com or you can contact me through facebook www.facebook.com/hopeleveltherapy.

I regularly add helpful information and updates on both sites, and you can find more information about my practice and how to book a session with me, as well as some downloadable hypnotherapeutic recordings that I have created to help with a range of issues.

I am happy to answer questions through the contact page on my website and am interested to hear about my readers experiences.

Any contact made with me will be treated in strictest confidence in accordance with my practice terms and conditions to ensure your safety.

I look forward to hearing from you,

Rachel x

www.hopeleveltherapy.com

ABOUT THE AUTHOR

Rachel May lives in Weardale with her partner Paul and a large assortment of dogs, cats and poultry. She is a qualified Integrative Hypnotherapeutic Psychotherapist and has been practicing since 2008. Rachel provides voluntary counselling to a Women's refuge and has worked with many victims of domestic violence. In her spare time, she enjoys leather craft and other artistic pursuits and has been threatening to write a fictional novel for more years than she can remember!

Rachel's current practice is an online service (www.hopeleveltherapy.com) which allows her clients to connect with her face to face irrespective of where they live. As well as the therapy sessions themselves, she also creates hypnotherapeutic recordings to complement her client based work. As an integrative therapist, Rachel draws on many different styles of therapy in order to provide a tailor made service to each client. She has worked with a huge range of people, (her list of clients range dramatically from age, race, gender, sexuality and culture) and includes both individuals and couples. This has allowed her to have a full understanding of a wide number of issues, and she believes that any issue that is causing someone distress is important, however small or hard to discuss. Rachel's greatest pleasure comes from helping people to enjoy living once more.

This book has been an extremely important mission, as it is as much her story of self-discovery as it is a guide for other people who are also struggling with the challenge of saying no, standing up for their own needs and putting themselves first. This is something which is at the core of what Rachel teaches.

ACKNOWLEDGEMENTS

I would like to thank everyone I have learned from, especially Tom Barber, Sandra Westland and their students at the Contemporary College for Therapeutic Studies, my mother and father, Jean and Roger who did a great job and my sister Rita, her husband Simon and of course my partner Paul and his family

I'd also like to thank the staff and and clients of Wear Valley Women's Refuge and my friend Garry who provided me with motivation and the drive to complete this project.

My thanks are also owed to Danielle for being a great editor and an extra special thank you to Alexa, my amazing publisher for keeping the faith, directing my focus and moving me forward.

REFERENCES & ADDITONAL SUPPORT

Games People Play: The Psychology of Human Relationships
Originally published: 1964
Author: Eric Berne
Publisher: Grove Press

Domestic violence in England and Wales BRIEFING PAPER Number 6337, 6 May 2016: By John Woodhouse and Noel Dempsey
www.parliament.uk/commons-library |
intranet.parliament.uk/commons-library | papers@parliament.uk |
@commonslibrary

National Health Service list of symptoms for NPD
http://www.nhs.uk/Conditions/Personalitydisorder/Pages/Symptoms
.aspx

Women's Aid – Recognising Domestic Abuse
https://www.womensaid.org.uk/information-support/what-is-
domestic-abuse/recognising-domestic-abuse/

Tom Barber and Sandra Westland
Contemporary College of Therapeutic Studies
https://contemporarycollege.com

Rachel May: www.hopeleveltherapy.com

I have also included some useful names, web addresses and phone numbers of UK support organisations on my website at www.hopeleveltherapy.com/emergency-help.